HAPPY
ORCHID

Project Editor Jo Whittingham

Designer Philippa Nash

Senior Editor Alastair Laing

Design assistance Mandy Earey, Karen Constanti

Picture Researcher Sakshi Saluja

Senior Jacket Creative Nicola Powling

Jacket Co-ordinator Lucy Philpott

Senior Producer (Pre-production) Tony Phipps

Senior Producer Ché Creasey

Creative Technical Support Sonia Charbonnier

Managing Editor Dawn Henderson

Managing Art Editor Marianne Markham

Art Director Maxine Pedliham

Publishing Director Mary-Clare Jerram

Illustrations Peter Bull

Photography Peter Anderson

First published in
Great Britain in 2018 by

Dorling Kindersley Limited,
80 Strand, London WC2R ORL

A CIP catalogue record for this book
is available from the British Library.
ISBN 978-0-2413-4922-9

Printed and bound in China.

**A WORLD OF IDEAS:
SEE ALL THERE IS TO KNOW
www.dk.com**

HAPPY ORCHID

HELP IT FLOWER, WATCH IT FLOURISH

SARA RITTERSHAUSEN

CONTENTS

FIND YOUR PLANT

With detailed information and care instructions for 143 gorgeous orchids, this section is packed with all the knowledge that you need to pamper your plants, and keep them flowering year after year.

TOP FIVE:

Easy-care *pp.52–53* • Weird and Wonderful *pp.70–71* • Beautifully Simple Display Ideas *pp.88–89* • Multi-plant Display Ideas *pp.106–107* • Hanging Display Ideas *pp.124–125*

COMET ORCHID
Angraecum sesquipedale
pp.34–35

TULIP ORCHID
Anguloa clowesii
pp.36–37

Angraecum **Crestwood**
p.35

Anguloa virginalis
p.37

Angraecum didieri
p.35

Angulocaste **Cotil Point**
p.37

Aspasia lunata
pp.38–39

SPIDER ORCHID
Brassia **Orange
Delight** *pp.42–43*

Bulbophyllum
**Elizabeth Ann
'Bucklebury'**
p.45

Calanthe tricarinata
p.47

Bletilla striata
pp.40–41

Brassia **Rex**
p.43

*Bulbophyllum
ambrosia*
p.45

CORSAGE ORCHID
Cattleya bowringiana
pp.48–49

Bletilla ochracea
p.41

Brassia
Ariana Verde
p.43

Calanthe discolor
pp.46–47

*Guarianthe
aurantiaca*
p.50

Bletilla striata alba
p.41

Bulbophyllum lobbii
pp.44–45

Calanthe striata
p.47

Cattleya bicolor
p.50

continued

Cattleya trianiae
p.51

Coelogyne flaccida
p.56

Coelogyne speciosa
p.57

Cymbidium goeringii
p.61

Cattleya forbesii
p.51

Coelogyne
massangeana
p.56

BOAT ORCHID
Cymbidium **Castle**
of Mey 'Pinkie'
pp.58–59

Cymbidium lowianum
p.61

Cattleya purpurata
p.51

Coelogyne mooreana
p.57

Cymbidium
erythraeum
p.60

Cymbidium
Sarah Jean
'Ice Cascade'
p.61

RAG ORCHID
Coelogyne cristata
pp.54–55

Coelogyne nitida
p.57

Cymbidium
erythrostylum
p.60

Dendrobium
Spring Dream
pp.62–63

Dendrobium
Comet King
p.63

Dendrobium
Emma Gold
p.65

PINEAPPLE ORCHID *Dendrobium densiflorum*
pp.68–69

Dendrobium
Irene Smile
p.63

Dendrobium
Berry Oda
pp.66–67

Dendrobium
infundibulum
p.69

Dendrochilum
cobbianum
p.73

Dendrobium
Polar Fire
pp.64–65

Dendrobium
kingianum
p.67

Dendrobium
williamsonii
p.69

Dendrochilum
wenzellii
p.73

Dendrobium **Sa-Nook**
Blue Happiness
p.65

Dendrobium speciosum
p.67

CHAIN ORCHID
Dendrochilum
glumaceum *pp.72–73*

TABLE MOUNTAIN
ORCHID *Disa uniflora*
pp.74–75

continued

Disa Diores
p. 75

Epicattleya
René Marqués
p. 79

JEWEL ORCHID
Ludisia discolor
pp. 82–83

Disa Kewensis
p. 75

Dracula vampira
p. 77

Laelia anceps
pp. 80–81

Lycaste aromatica
pp. 84–85

Dracula bella
pp. 76–77

CRUCIFIX ORCHID
Epidendrum radicans
pp. 78–79

Laelia gouldiana
p. 81

Lycaste virginalis
p. 85

Dracula simia
p. 77

Epidendrum porpax
p. 79

Laelia autumnalis
p. 81

Lycaste deppei
p. 85

KITE ORCHID
Masdevallia coccinea
pp.86–87

Maxillaria coccinea
p.92

Maxillaria variabilis
p.93

PANSY ORCHID
Miltoniopsis
Herralexandre
pp.96–97

Masdevallia
barlaeana
p.87

Maxillaria
meleagris
p.92

Miltonia Sunset
pp.94–95

Miltoniopsis
Red Tide
p.97

Masdevallia coriacea
p.87

Maxillaria picta
p.93

Miltonia spectabilis
p.95

Miltoniopsis
Pink Cadillac
p.97

Maxillaria praestans
pp.90–91

Maxillaria tenuifolia
p.93

Miltonia flavescens
p.95

DANCING LADIES
Oncidium Sweet Sugar
pp.98–99

continued

*Oncidium
cheirophorum*
p.100

*Oncidium
unguiculatum*
p.101

Oncidium
Mieke Von Holm
p.105

*Paphiopedilum
callosum*
p.110

*Oncidium
ornithorhynchum*
p.100

CAMBRIA ORCHID
Oncidopsis
Nelly Isler
pp.102–103

Oncostele
Catatante
p.105

*Paphiopedilum
delenatii*
p.110

Oncidium
Sharry Baby
p.101

Aliceara
Peggy Ruth
Carpenter
p.104

Oncostele
Midnight Miracles
'Massai Red'
p.105

Paphiopedilum
Pinocchio
p.111

Oncidium
Twinkle
p.101

Aliceara
Tahoma Glacier
p.104

SLIPPER ORCHID
Paphiopedilum Maudiae
pp.108–109

*Paphiopedilum
sukhakulii*
p.111

Paphiopedilum wardii
p.111

*Phalaenopsis
equestris*
p.117

*Phragmipedium
Sedenii*
p.119

SLIPPER ORCHID
*Paphiopedilum
insigne*
pp.112–113

MOTH ORCHID
*Phalaenopsis
Cool Breeze*
pp.114–115

*Phalaenopsis
Happy Minho*
p.117

*Phragmipedium
Grande*
p.119

*Paphiopedilum
Leeanum*
p.113

*Phalaenopsis
Atlantis*
p.116

*Phalaenopsis
Limelight*
p.117

Pleione formosana
pp.120–121

*Paphiopedilum
villosum*
p.113

*Phalaenopsis
cornu-cervi*
p.116

SLIPPER ORCHID
Phragmipedium besseae
pp.118–119

*Pleione
bulbocodioides*
p.122

continued

Pleione formosana var. alba
p.122

OCTOPUS ORCHID
Prosthechea cochleata
pp.128–129

Restrepia gutullata
p.131

Pleione
Piton
p.123

*Pleurothallis
restrepioides*
pp.126–127

Prosthechea radiata
p.129

Restrepia brachypus
p.131

Pleione pleionoides
p.123

Pleurothallis truncata
p.127

Prosthechea garciana
p.129

**UPSIDE-DOWN
ORCHID**
Stanhopea tigrina
pp.132–133

Pleione
Shantung
p.123

*Pleurothallis
palliolata*
p.127

Restrepia cuprea
pp.130–131

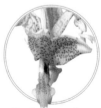

Stanhopea oculata
p.133

Stanhopea graveolens
p.133

Vanda
Yellow Magic
p.139

Thunia
Gattonensis
pp.134–135

Vanda
Blue Magic
pp.136–137

Zygopetalum
Artur Elle
pp.140–141

Thunia marshalliana
p.135

Vanda
Exotic Purple
p.138

Vanda
Pink Magic
p.139

Zygopetalum
crinitum
p.141

Thunia alba
p.135

Vanda
Rothschildiana
p.138

Vanda
Princess Mikasa Blue
p.139

Zygopetalum mackayi
p.141

THE BASICS

THE WORLD OF ORCHIDS

The orchid family is the world's largest group of flowering plants, with around 30,000 species, and over 120,000 hybrids. Once grown only by enthusiasts, many are now easily available, and make ideal houseplants.

GROWING IN THE WILD

Orchids grow in, and have become perfectly adapted to, an incredible range of habitats, from tropical rainforests in Central America, Africa, and Asia, to semi-arid regions in Australia, and temperate grassland in Europe. They often thrive where other plants struggle: clinging to trees or rocks, surviving cold weather at high altitudes, or happy in lowland heat.

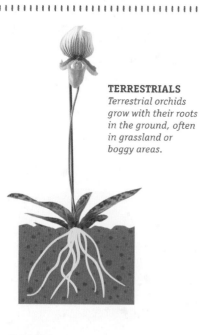

TERRESTRIALS
Terrestrial orchids grow with their roots in the ground, often in grassland or boggy areas.

EPIPHYTES
Many tropical orchids flourish in the branches of trees as epiphytes. Rather than taking nutrients from the tree, their fleshy aerial roots anchor them, and absorb moisture from the air.

GROWTH HABITS

Understanding whether your orchid has a monopodial or sympodial growth habit is valuable, because it affects the way that it grows and flowers, and how it can be propagated.

Fleshy roots are produced from the rhizome

Each year new shoots spread sideways to fill the pot

Growth is made upwards rather than outwards

SYMPODIAL ORCHIDS
These orchids spread by a horizontal rhizome to form clumps of leaves, often with swollen pseudobulbs beneath them for storing water. Flowers usually arise from the newest growth.

MONOPODIAL ORCHIDS
These orchids produce new leaves from a central crown, which means the orchid grows taller each year in a single direction. The flower stems grow from between the leaves.

FLOWER STRUCTURE

Orchid flowers are extremely variable in size, colour, and shape, but they all share the same, symmetrical structure which you will quickly start to recognize.

2 petals

Column tipped with pollen cap

Protruding lip, formed by 3rd petal

3 sepals

CHOOSING AND BUYING PLANTS

Selecting the right orchid to thrive in your home, and finding a plant in good condition, are both important first steps to success. Here are a few simple tips to help you choose the perfect, healthy orchid to take home.

RELIABLE SOURCES

Orchids are now widely available at low prices online and in many supermarkets. These plants are not always named, however, and may not have been properly cared for. If you're looking for a healthy orchid that will flower repeatedly, try to buy from an orchid nursery or garden centre. An orchid specialist is a must if you're after something more unusual. Be cautious with online traders, as plants may be incorrectly labelled, not as described, or not even orchids at all.

Dendrobium **Berry Oda (pp.66–67)**

THINGS TO CONSIDER

☑ **Where will I grow it?**
Some orchids prefer the warmth found in a lounge or kitchen, while others enjoy a cooler room. Choose a plant that will suit its position.

☑ **How much space do I have?**
Where space is limited, there are many compact and miniature orchids to choose from. Larger orchids are spectacular, if you can spare the room.

☑ **Do I want an orchid that's easy to grow?**
Starting with something easy builds up your confidence and skills. Build on your success by moving onto more challenging orchids.

☑ **Would I like the flowers to have scent?**
Fragrance can be a lovely addition to the flowers, but some orchids have strong scents that are not always sweet. Make sure you sniff before you buy!

☑ **Do I want it to flower in a particular season?**
Some orchids bloom at specific times of year, but others flower more randomly. Check the profiles, and seek advice from specialist nurseries.

BEFORE YOU BUY

When choosing your orchid, check it is a healthy plant with plump leaves, pseudobulbs, and roots. Wilted or yellow leaves, shrivelled pseudobulbs, and brown roots are all signs that a plant has not been properly cared for. Flowers should be fresh, with more buds still to open. Avoid plants with drooping flowers and yellow buds, because these may have been caused by extremes of temperature.

TRAVELLING HOME

Avoid exposing your new orchid to extremes of weather. Do not leave the plant in a hot car, because the heat will damage it. In cold weather, make sure your plant is wrapped in a plastic sleeve, or paper, to protect it from being chilled on the journey home. Secure orchids with long flower stems before moving the car, so that they do not tip over.

Look for fresh blooms and buds

Plump pseudobulbs indicate good health

Dendrobium **Polar Fire (pp.64–65)**

Take care not to damage long flower stems

Wrap in paper to keep warm

Pansy orchid (pp.96–97)

POTTING AND PLANTING

When your new orchid arrives home, check that it is healthy, and potted correctly, before putting it on display. Once its roots are in a suitable container, caring for your orchid will be simple.

CHECK THE POT

Most orchids should not require repotting until after flowering, but look out for problems. Check the pot has drainage holes: if not, the compost will be soggy, the roots will be turning brown, and immediate repotting is required. Roots curling around the inside of the pot, or a top-heavy plant that tips over easily, also mean that a new pot is needed.

Table mountain orchid (pp.74–75)

CHOOSE A POT

If you decide that your orchid needs a new container, then take care to select one that will provide the ideal conditions for its roots.

• **The new pot** should only be one or two sizes larger than the original, making sure that there is 2cm (¾in) between the plant and the edge of the pot. A pot that is too large will lead to overwatering. Clear plastic pots help you to see the health of the roots. Clay pots are attractive, but porous, and dry out faster.

• **Good drainage** is the most important attribute in a new pot, because orchids do not like their roots sitting in water. Choose a pot with plenty of drainage holes in the base, and even the sides too; that way the compost will not get too wet, and the roots are much less likely to rot.

New, larger pot

Pot drainage holes

PLANTING

To repot your orchid, remove it from its old pot, clear the compost from its roots, and cut off any dead roots. Position the roots in the new pot, and fill with free-draining chipped bark, unless directed differently in the orchid's profile. Plastic pots can be placed in a slightly larger decorative cover pot if you wish, but be sure not to leave the orchid standing in water.

Lower roots into the pot and add chipped bark

Firm roots into a new pot

Choose a slightly larger cover pot

See Repotting (pp.26–27)

STAKING

If your orchid has a tall, upright growth habit, like many dendrobiums (see pp.62–67), attach the canes to stakes, to support the plant. Long flower stems can also benefit from staking, which helps to prevent the stems breaking under the weight of heavy flowers.

COMPOST

Chipped bark is a good all-round, free-draining compost for most orchids, but other options are recommended for those that prefer more moisture.

Bark: fine grade
Smaller pieces of bark, for miniature or young plants, eg *Pleione*.

Bark: medium grade
A good general grade for most potted orchids, eg *Oncidium*.

Bark: coarse grade
Chunky pieces for orchids that require extra drainage, eg *Cattleya*.

Houseplant compost/coir
Combine with bark to hold moisture for damp-growing orchids, eg *Bletilla*.

Rockwool
Moisture-retentive compost for orchids that like to be wet, eg *Phragmipedium*.

Sphagnum moss
Used fresh or rehydrated: ideal for miniatures, eg *Masdevallia*.

Coconut fibre
A denser compost that suits terrestrial orchids, eg *Paphiopedilum*.

POSITION AND HUMIDITY

To thrive, each orchid needs to be grown in its preferred temperature range, and with the right levels of light and humidity. Creating an environment that reflects the plant's native habitat will allow it to flourish.

LOCATION

Choosing the right spot for your orchid is an important step to success. Some like bright and warm positions, while others prefer shady and cool. Check your orchid's individual profile, and don't be afraid to move them seasonally, to provide lower temperatures, and more light in winter.

TEMPERATURE

Orchids usually require one of three temperature ranges: cool 10–20°C (50–68°F), intermediate 12–22°C (54–72°F), or warm 15–25°C (59–77°F). This 10°C (18°F) difference between winter nights and summer days encourages flowering. Reduce summer heat with good shade, ventilation, and humidity. Maintain warmth in winter by keeping in a heated room.

LIGHT

Plentiful light helps orchids flower, but bright, direct, summer sun burns their delicate leaves. Find them a summer position close to a north-facing window, where the sun is naturally weaker, or provide some shade with blinds or netting. Foliage can withstand direct winter sun, so move to a south-facing window for winter.

Miltonia Sunset (pp.94–95)

HUMIDITY

Many orchids originate from the rainforest, so to keep them happy it's necessary to create humidity, because the atmosphere of your centrally heated home will be dry. Some rooms, such as bathrooms and kitchens, are usually more humid, and there are several simple ways to increase humidity elsewhere.

HYDROLECA TRAY

Standing pots on a tray of porous clay pellets, such as hydroleca, which are kept sprayed with water, allows moisture to evaporate around your orchids. This increases local humidity, and combats a dry atmosphere indoors. Keep the hydroleca moist at all times, but do not allow pots to stand in water, or sink into the pellets, in case the roots become too wet.

Moist clay pellets increase humidity

Zygopetalum Artur Elle (pp.140–141)

MISTING

Create humidity by misting your orchid's leaves and roots regularly. Use a small hand sprayer to provide a fine mist of water and keep it next to your plants. Mist daily during warm weather, and less often at cooler times, but always in the morning to allow evaporation during the day. Use rainwater or soft water, as hard water coats leaves with lime deposits.

Spray your orchid's roots and leaves

Spider orchid (pp.42–43)

CREATE A MICROCLIMATE

Growing orchids together with other houseplants, like bromeliads and ferns, creates a mini-microclimate and increases the humidity surrounding the plants.

Display plants in attractive groups

ORCHID CARE

Orchids are tough plants, often adapted to live in challenging conditions, so caring for them is easy and undemanding when you know the few simple rules to follow.

FLOWERING

Strong, healthy orchids produce the best blooms. The way to encourage flowering is to water and feed your plant correctly, so that its leaves and pseudobulbs grow and mature enough to form blooms each year. Ensuring that there are seasonal changes in temperature, and good winter light, also helps orchids to flower reliably.

Consistent care leads to perfect flowers

Moth orchid (pp.114–115)

WATERING

Most orchids need to be watered from the top of the pot. Roots that are constantly wet become prone to rotting, so allow them to dry out before watering again. Check the pot weekly, and remember that it's better to err on the drier side. Submerge very dry pots for 10–20 minutes to rewet the compost, but never leave them standing in water. Use soft water or rainwater, as hard water deposits lime in the compost. Some orchids need a winter rest, with little watering, while others prefer much damper conditions. Check each orchid's profile for its individual needs.

Allow water to run through the compost

Water from above

FEEDING

Epiphytic orchids live in the trees, where the only nutrients available come from decomposing leaf litter dissolved in rainwater. This means that pot-grown orchids do not need to be fed very often, and that it's best to use specialist orchid feeds.

HOW TO FEED

Add fertilizer to water as directed on the label, and apply every 2–3 waterings. Always flush the pot with plain water in between feeds, to prevent a build up of salts in the compost. Fertilizers can also be sprayed onto the leaves, which is an easy way to feed a few plants. Ready-to-use sprays are usually a weaker dilution, and so can be used to feed weekly.

Use a liquid "bloom" feed

Add feed when watering

DIFFERENT FEEDS

Using the correct fertilizer for each stage of your orchid's growth cycle will produce the best results.
High-nitrogen "grow" feed boosts new leaf and pseudobulb growth, and should be used when your orchid's leaves are actively growing.
High-potash "bloom" feed helps mature new leaves and pseudobulbs, and promote the production of flowers. Use it towards the end of the growing season, when leaves and pseudobulbs are a good size, and during flowering to prolong the display.

REGULAR CARE

Orchids are happiest, and look their best, when kept clean and tidy.

● Keep leaves dust-free and shiny by wiping weekly with a soft damp cloth.

● Remove any dead leaves, or brown roots to prevent them rotting.

● Trim off brown leaf tips. Check that watering and light levels are suitable.

● Deadhead flowers, and remove fallen flowers to keep the plant and pot tidy.

● Trim off dead, brown flower stems that have finished blooming.

REPOTTING

Orchids that are flourishing will outgrow their container every few years, and need moving into a larger pot. Repotting is a simple process when you follow the easy steps below.

WHEN TO REPOT

It is best to repot your orchid every 2–3 years, because after this time it is likely to have filled its pot, and the compost will be starting to deteriorate.

☑ Check if the plant is "pot bound". If the pot is full of healthy roots, choose a pot two sizes larger to allow them more space.

☑ Plants that are spilling over the edge of the pot, or have become top-heavy need more room. Repot when new leaves and/or pseudobulbs fill the top of the pot.

☑ Repot immediately if roots have turned brown and rotted because of overwatering. The compost will be waterlogged, and needs to be replaced.

☑ The best times to repot are after your orchid has flowered, in the spring, or when the plant is actively growing.

Some orchids spread to "climb" out of their pot

An orchid that has become pot bound

HOW TO REPOT

Although monopodial and sympodial orchids look different, the method for repotting them is the same. A monopodial orchid is shown here. Sympodial orchids usually spread faster and need moving on more often.

1 Water the day before repotting. Choose a new pot 2 sizes larger, with plenty of drainage holes in its base. A clear pot enables you to see the roots.

2 Add a layer of broken terracotta or chips of polystyrene for extra drainage. Cover with a little damp compost of the type stated in the orchid profile.

3 Remove the orchid from its pot, and clean the old compost from its roots. Trim off any dead, or extra-long roots, keeping them 8–10cm (3–4in) in length.

4 Position the orchid in its new pot so its leaves will sit on the surface of the compost. Add more compost if needed. Rigid aerial roots can be left outside the pot.

5 Hold in position and fill around the roots with compost, to just below the pot's rim. Secure by pushing the bark down with your thumbs, or a potting stick.

6 Water within 24 hours of repotting, and check the pot a few days later, as newly potted plants can dry out quickly to start with. Mist daily as usual.

PROPAGATING

Try propagating from your favourite orchid to make more plants for yourself, or to share. Although not every orchid propagates easily, many are simple to multiply using division or keikis.

KEIKIS

A few orchids can form baby plants, called keikis: a Hawaiian word for "little one". These can easily be potted up to create new plants.

DENDROBIUMS

Keikis can grow on tall *Dendrobium* canes. Remove and pot up the keiki once it has grown a small, plumped-up pseudobulb and some roots of its own. Plants usually produce keikis when they have been kept too warm and wet during the winter resting season. Keikis are formed instead of flower buds, so it is preferable not to have too many.

Carefully cut away the keiki

Dendrobium Spring Dream (pp.62–63)

MOTH ORCHIDS

These orchids are able to produce keikis from the eyes along the length of their flower stems. When the keiki has grown a few leaves, and several roots at least 5cm (2in) long, then carefully remove it and pot it up. Keikis can form randomly, but they occur more often if the plant has been overfed, or kept too hot.

Keikis are identical clones of the parent plant

Moth orchid (pp.114–115)

DIVIDING SYMPODIAL ORCHIDS

Only sympodial orchids with a spreading habit can be propagated by division. Divide an orchid when it becomes too large, or to create several new plants. Wait until after flowering, as it starts into growth.

1 Remove the orchid from its pot, clean the old compost from around roots, and trim off any dead or excessively long roots. Tidy up any dead leaves.

2 Look carefully to decide where to divide it. Divisions with at least four pseudobulbs, and one new growth, will be able to flower the following season.

3 Gently pull divisions apart, or cut using a sharp knife or secateurs. Older pseudobulbs, known as backbulbs, need extra care and time to flower.

4 Select new pots with enough space for each division to grow for 2–3 years. Add polystyrene chips or broken terracotta for extra drainage.

5 Place each division in its pot, with its new growth at what will be the compost level. Hold in position, fill around the roots with bark chips, and firm down well.

6 Water within 24 hours of being potted, and check a few days later, as newly potted plants can dry out quickly to start with. Mist daily as usual.

PESTS AND PROBLEMS

Orchids are not usually troubled by many problems, but some are prone to a few common insect pests, and all will encounter difficulties in unsuitable growing conditions.

PREVENTING PESTS

By keeping a close eye on your orchids you will quickly notice any pests, and be able to deal with them promptly. Keep any affected plants quarantined from healthy plants until the pest is cleared. It is good practice to mist regularly, wipe leaves on both sides to keep them clean, and remove any dying flowers and leaves, which can harbour pests.

RED SPIDER MITE

These microscopic mites enjoy warm, dry conditions, and occur on boat and pansy orchids in hot rooms. Watch for silvery black spots on leaves, particularly underneath older foliage.

TREAT IT

♥ *Keep susceptible plants cool and humid. Mist regularly above and below the leaves, and wipe them with a damp cloth at least once a month.*

MEALYBUG

A white, fluffy insect found hiding around flowers, and between and under leaves, especially on moth orchids. Left untreated they multiply rapidly, so tackle promptly to prevent a troublesome infestation.

TREAT IT

♥ *Remove affected flowers and leaves, then clean remaining leaves with a small brush dipped in methylated spirits, which kills the insects on contact. Check and treat the whole plant, the pot, and other containers and saucers. If bugs are found in the compost, they can be treated with a systemic insecticide spray, and the plant repotted.*

Mealybug infestation

SCALE INSECT

These insects hide under a hard, round, yellow-brown scale, and can be found in between leaves and stems, and in any other crevices. They can occur on most orchids, but most commonly on corsage and boat orchids.

TREAT IT

♥ *Check the plant thoroughly, then clean leaves with a small brush dipped in methylated spirits, and gently scrub off the scale insects. The plant can also be sprayed with a systemic insecticide, and repotted into fresh compost, to remove the risk of pests hiding in the pot.*

APHIDS

Greenfly are the main aphid to affect orchids, and are commonly found on flowers, buds, and young leaf shoots. They come in from outside through open doors and windows, especially in warm weather.

TREAT IT

♥ *Do not treat flowers and buds with any strong chemicals: simply wash the aphids off them, and young leaves, with water mixed with a little washing up detergent. Nectar from flowers attracts aphids. If it drips onto leaves, wipe them clean.*

RESOLVING PROBLEMS

These problems are usually associated with incorrect growing conditions, so take care to avoid overwatering, excessive light, and extremes of temperature.

BUD DROP

Flower buds can drop before opening, due to extremes in temperature, either chilling or heating, which have put the plant under stress.

TREAT IT

♥ *Trim off the flower stem, and move the plant to a better spot. Trim moth orchid stems back to a healthy eye, and they may quickly form new buds.*

ROOT ROT

Brown, spongy roots have rotted as a result of watering too frequently. The leaves of waterlogged plants will turn yellow.

TREAT IT

♥ *Trim back any dead and rotten roots, and repot the plant promptly into fresh compost. Keep warm and humid to encourage new root growth, and only water when the compost has dried out.*

Rotten brown roots

ORCHID
PROFILES

COMET ORCHID

Angraecum sesquipedale

During winter and spring, these spectacular, star-shaped flowers each trail an impressive 30cm (12in) spur, which has been likened to the tail of a comet. As natives of rainforests, they flourish given high humidity.

VITAL STATISTICS

HOW IT GROWS
As a monopodial epiphyte, which anchors itself to the branch of a tree with its aerial roots.

ORIGIN
Native to the rainforests of Madagascar.

ANATOMY
Forms an upright fan of thick leaves. Flower stems each carry 1–4 large, waxy blooms, and emerge from between leaves.

SIZE Foliage can reach 30cm (12in) tall, and spread to 40cm (16in) wide. The slender, flower stems, grow up to 40cm (16in) tall, and often arch downwards.

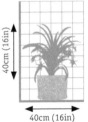

40cm (16in)

40cm (16in)

WATER
Check weekly and water from the top of the pot when the compost is dry. To prevent roots rotting, allow excess water to drain and never stand in water. Create humidity by misting the leaves and roots daily.

POSITION
Thrives given a bright position, shaded from the summer sun, in a warm room with a winter minimum of 18°C (64°F). Try a south-facing bathroom for extra humidity.

HELP TO FLOWER

High humidity and good light encourage flowering in winter and spring. Once the flowers have faded, trim the dead stem back and a brand new flowering stem will emerge from between the leaves.

FEED

Boost new spring and summer growth with a high-nitrogen fertilizer every 2–3 waterings. Mature this growth and promote flowering with a high-potash fertilizer in late summer and autumn. No feeding is required in winter.

REPOT

Aim to repot every 2–3 years, using coarse bark chippings, when the plant has become top heavy and filled its pot with roots. Aerial roots are not necessarily a sign that repotting is required.

THE RELATIVES

Other *Angraecum* from Madagascan and African rainforests thrive in the same conditions, but vary in size.

ANGRAECUM CRESTWOOD
A hybrid of A. sesquipedale, which is more vigorous, and produces even more large, pure white flowers.

ANGRAECUM DIDIERI
This white-flowered, miniature species only grows to around 10cm (4in) across and thrives mounted on a piece of bark.

TULIP ORCHID

Anguloa clowesii

Large, rounded pseudobulbs give rise to long-lasting, waxy, highly fragrant flowers and impressive broad leaves, which grow through summer, but fall naturally from this deciduous orchid in autumn.

VITAL STATISTICS

HOW IT GROWS This orchid has a sympodial habit, and is usually found growing as a terrestrial in damp ground.

ORIGIN Native to high altitudes in Colombia and Venezuela.

ANATOMY Forms a cluster of large pseudobulbs with broad, deciduous leaves. Single, strongly scented flowers shoot up from the base.

SIZE Can reach 80cm (32in) high and spread to 50cm (20in) wide in leaf. Smaller when dormant. Flowers stand up to 50cm (20in) tall.

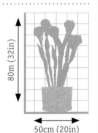

80m (32in)

50cm (20in)

WATER

When new growth starts in spring, water weekly into summer to boost the new pseudobulbs. Once the summer leaves have dropped, only water if the pseudobulbs start to wrinkle. Stop watering during winter to provide a period of dry rest.

POSITION

In spring and summer, keep as cool as possible (below 20°C /68°F) and shade the soft leaves to prevent direct sunlight burning them. Place in a cool, unheated room during winter, where the temperature drops to 10°C (50°F) at night.

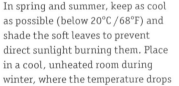

HELP TO FLOWER

A cool winter rest and strong summer growth both promote good blooms. After flowering, trim the dead stems back to the base of the plant.

FEED

Fuel new growth with a high-nitrogen fertilizer every 2–3 waterings throughout spring and summer. Use a high-potash fertilizer in late summer and autumn to mature the growth and encourage flowering. Do not feed in winter.

REPOT

Large new pseudobulbs are produced each year, which will fill the pot quickly. Repot every 1–2 years in summer after flowering, using a mix of fine bark, perlite, and sphagnum moss.

THE RELATIVES

All species of *Anguloa* are deciduous, cool-growing, and need a winter rest. They are also often scented.

ANGULOA VIRGINALIS
A more forward-facing flower, but still tulip-like, in white or soft pink with darker pink patterning inside. Originates from South America.

ANGULOCASTE COTIL POINT
The amazing textured and heavily scented flowers of this hybrid have a tulip-like shape, but unfurl their petals like their Lycaste parent.

ASPASIA LUNATA

Easy to cultivate and free-flowering, Aspasia lunata is ideal for beginners looking to try their hand at growing a species orchid, and its diminutive size means it won't take up too much space on the windowsill.

VITAL STATISTICS

HOW IT GROWS This orchid has a sympodial habit, and grows as an epiphyte on the branches of trees, anchored by strong aerial roots.

ORIGIN Native to the tropical forests of Brazil and Bolivia.

ANATOMY Produces oval, flattened pseudobulbs, each topped with a pair of short leaves. A rhizome connects the pseudobulbs, giving the plants a creeping habit.

SIZE Foliage grows to 30cm (12in) high and will spread to 20cm (8in) or more. Flowers are produced at the tips of short stems 10cm (4in) tall.

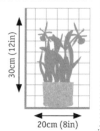

30cm (12in)

20cm (8in)

WATER
Water from the top of the pot and drain well so the pot never stands in water. In spring and summer water weekly, reducing to every 2–3 weeks in autumn and winter. Allow compost to dry out in between waterings.

POSITION
Suits a shaded position with an intermediate temperature range of 12–22°C (54–72°F). Don't allow winter temperatures to dip lower. Try a humid bathroom or kitchen window, where leaves can be misted daily.

HELP TO FLOWER

Given warm temperatures and daily misting of the leaves, blooms will appear in autumn. When flowers fade, trim the short dead stems back to the base.

FEED

In spring and summer, a high-nitrogen fertilizer every 2–3 waterings encourages new growth, while a high potash-fertilizer in late summer and autumn matures growth and promotes flowering. Do not feed during winter.

REPOT

It is time to repot when the new pseudobulbs have reached the edge of the pot. This can be necessary every 2–3 years, or more often if a plant is thriving. Use medium or coarse bark chippings.

"Suits a temperature range of 12–22°C (54–72°F). Don't allow winter temperatures to dip lower."

BLETILLA STRIATA

Stand this showy orchid outdoors in summer and bring inside to avoid any winter frosts. It puts on a great display of flowers in spring and early summer, then drops its leaves in winter for a well-earned rest.

VITAL STATISTICS

HOW IT GROWS A sympodial orchid, which is found growing as a terrestrial in damp soil. Its spreading habit allows it to form attractive clusters of foliage.

ORIGIN Native to shady woodland in Japan, China, and Korea.

ANATOMY Forms pseudobulbs below ground, which multiply in summer to form a clump. New shoots produce a flower stem from their centre.

SIZE Flower stems can reach 60cm (24in), held above the 40cm (16in) long, narrow leaves. Plants can easily reach a width of 20cm (8in).

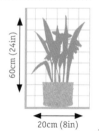

60cm (24in)

20cm (8in)

WATER

Begin watering weekly when the new shoots grow in spring, and continue through summer to promote the growth of new, underground pseudobulbs. Stop watering once the leaves have dropped, to give the plant a dry winter rest.

POSITION

A shady spot outdoors in the garden is ideal in spring and summer. Direct sunlight may burn the leaves, but come autumn they will drop anyway. Before frosts arrive, move to a conservatory or cool porch, which is frost-free but light, for the winter rest.

HELP TO FLOWER

Feed and water during spring and early summer, to produce new flowering shoots. Trim back dead stems.

FEED

Add a high-nitrogen fertilizer to the water every 2–3 waterings throughout spring and summer to boost the new pseudobulbs' growth. Switch to a high-potash fertilizer in late summer and autumn to mature growth and encourage flowering. Stop feeding in winter.

REPOT

Carry out annual repotting in spring, when the new shoots emerge. Remove old compost along with any older, dead pseudobulbs,and repot with a mix of fine bark, perlite, and houseplant compost to keep the roots moist all summer.

THE RELATIVES

All the orchids from the small *Bletilla* group are deciduous and enjoy the same cold conditions.

BLETILLA OCHRACEA
A species from Vietnam and China, with creamy yellow flowers and markings on the lip. Also happy growing outdoors.

BLETILLA STRIATA ALBA
This charming form of B. striata is easy to grow, and has pure white flowers, which shine in a shady spot.

SPIDER ORCHID

Brassia Orange Delight

This exotic-looking orchid is thought to resemble a spider with its long, orange petals and spotted lip. Its compact habit and ease of cultivation make this hybrid a popular choice for beginners.

VITAL STATISTICS

HOW IT GROWS As a sympodial epiphyte on the branches of trees, with strong aerial roots to anchor it.

ORIGIN Native to Central America, Venezuela, and northern Brazil.

ANATOMY Forms a spreading rhizome with large, oval pseudobulbs, each producing a pair of broad leaves from the tip, and a flower stem from the side.

SIZE Leaves can grow up to 30cm (12in) high, and the arching flower stems reach the same height. In time plants can spread to 50cm (20in) wide.

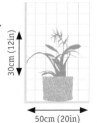

30cm (12in)

50cm (20in)

WATER

Water from the top of the pot and allow to drain well, never standing the pot in water. Allow to dry out well in between waterings, and water weekly during spring and summer growth, and every 2–3 weeks in autumn and winter.

POSITION

Needs intermediate temperatures, from 12°C (54°F) in a bright position in winter, to a maximum of 22°C (72°F) in summer, in good, indirect light to stop leaves burning. Try a humid bathroom, where leaves can be misted regularly.

HELP TO FLOWER

Good light and humidity will encourage flowering each year, usually in summer. When the flowers have died, trim the dead stems back to the base.

FEED

Apply a high-nitrogen fertilizer every 2–3 waterings during growth, which usually occurs in winter. Use a high-potash fertilizer to mature growth during spring and promote flowering.

REPOT

Use medium or coarse bark chippings to repot when the pseudobulbs have reached the edge of the pot. This is usually necessary every 2–3 years, but sometimes more often for fast-growing plants.

THE RELATIVES

The many *Brassia* hybrids have a range of long-petalled, spidery flowers in shades and patterns of green and red.

BRASSIA REX
A bigger, more robust hybrid than B. Orange Delight, with 6–8 large, green and maroon flowers on a tall, arching stem.

BRASSIA ARIANA VERDE
Long stems packed with yellow-green flowers, each dramatically marked with dark red, make this larger hybrid extremely striking.

BULBOPHYLLUM LOBBII

Given warmth, this makes an easy and dramatic addition to a beginner's collection, with striking yellow summer flowers and a sprawling habit well-suited to a hanging basket.

VITAL STATISTICS

HOW IT GROWS As a sympodial epiphyte on the branch or trunk of a tree, with aerial roots to anchor it.

ORIGIN From Borneo, Indonesia, the Philippines, and Malaysia.

ANATOMY The creeping rhizomes produce rounded pseudobulbs, each with one leathery leaf. A single flower tops each stem.

SIZE Leaves and flower stems of mature plants can both reach 40cm (16in) high. Plants will sprawl to 30cm (12in) wide in time.

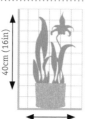

40cm (16in)

30cm (12in)

WATER

Water from the top of the pot and allow to dry out throughly between waterings, never leaving the plant standing in water. In spring and summer, water weekly, reducing to every 2–3 weeks in autumn and winter.

POSITION

Shield from direct summer sunlight in a north-facing room, moving into sunlight during winter. Choose a warm room, such as a kitchen or lounge, with a maximum summer temperature of 25°C (77°F) and a minimum of 15°C (59°F) at night.

FEED

Plants producing new growth in spring and summer need a high-nitrogen fertilizer every 2–3 waterings. Switch to a high-potash fertilizer in late summer and autumn to mature the growth and encourage flowering. No feeding is required in winter.

HELP TO FLOWER

Warm conditions and consistent watering through spring and summer will produce summer blooms each year. Trim spent flower stems to the base.

REPOT

Use medium or coarse bark chippings to repot, when new pseudobulbs have reached the edge of the pot. This is usually necessary every 2–3 years, but wait until after flowering when new leaf shoots show.

THE RELATIVES

The bizarre flowers of this large genus come in many shapes and sizes. These examples thrive in the same conditions as *B. lobbii*.

***BULBOPHYLLUM* ELIZABETH ANN 'BUCKLEBURY'**
A beautiful hybrid, with semi-circular sprays of long-tailed pink flowers hanging down from each arching stem.

BULBOPHYLLUM AMBROSIA
Subtly coloured and smaller-flowered, this creeping, clump-forming species is suited to viewing from a hanging pot, like many of its relatives.

CALANTHE DISCOLOR

Tall stems of delicate bicoloured flowers suit the cool shade enjoyed by this hardy species, which flourishes in a cold conservatory or greenhouse.

VITAL STATISTICS

HOW IT GROWS As a sympodial terrestrial in damp, shady rainforest at low altitude, close to streams and springs.

ORIGIN Native to China, Japan, and Korea.

ANATOMY Produces broad, soft leaves from underground pseudobulbs. Stems bearing flowers emerge from new rosettes of leaves.

SIZE Rosettes of leaves can reach 30cm (12in) high and 20cm (8in) wide, with flower stems up to 50cm (20in) tall.

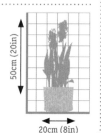

50cm (20in)

20cm (8in)

WATER

Water weekly in spring and summer when in leaf, ensuring that the roots are kept moist throughout the growing season, but keep drier in winter once the leaves have dropped. Water from the top and allow to drain.

POSITION

Keep in a cold room, such as an unheated porch or conservatory, with shading to protect the foliage from direct summer sunlight. These tough orchids are hardy to -5°C (23°F), so could also be grown outdoors.

HELP TO FLOWER

Ensuring that plants receive cold, dry winter conditions will promote blooms in spring and summer. When the last flowers finally fade, trim off the dead flower stem.

FEED

Apply a high-nitrogen fertilizer every 2–3 waterings during spring and summer growth. Use a high-potash fertilizer in late summer and autumn to encourage flowering.

REPOT

Repot or plant out in early spring when the new shoots start to grow. Use an organic compost that retains moisture well.

THE RELATIVES

Both of these *Calanthe* grow well in cool conditions, given plenty of shade, and are hardy to -5°C (23°F).

CALANTHE STRIATA
A spectacular species, producing a graceful spike of long-lasting, bright yellow flowers, which is from Japan, Korea, and Taiwan.

CALANTHE TRICARINATA
An attractive green flower with dark red on the lip, from Pakistan in the west across the Himalayas to Japan in the east.

48

Orchid profiles

CORSAGE ORCHID

Cattleya bowringiana

Given warm growing conditions, and the right seasonal light levels, this orchid will produce large, delicately scented blooms. These glamorous, long-lasting flowers were once popular corsages among Hollywood stars.

VITAL STATISTICS

HOW IT GROWS As a sympodial epiphyte on the branches of trees, with strong aerial roots to anchor it.

ORIGIN Native to Guatemala and Belize.

ANATOMY Rhizomes grow horizontally, and form elongated, oval pseudobulbs, from which emerge one or two leathery leaves, and a sheath of 2–4 flower buds.

SIZE Foliage can reach 45cm (18in) wide and 60cm (24in) high, with flowers up to 8cm (3in) across sitting just above the leaves.

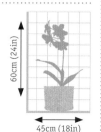

60cm (24in)

45cm (18in)

WATER

Water from the top of the pot and allow to drain well; do not stand in water. Allow to dry out well between waterings. Plants may require water weekly in spring and summer, and every 2–3 weeks in autumn and winter.

FEED

Boost new growth throughout spring and summer by applying a high-nitrogen fertilizer every 2–3 waterings. Move to a high-potash fertilizer in late summer and autumn to mature the growth and encourage flowering. Feeding is not required in winter.

HELP TO FLOWER

Keep plants in good light, and dry during winter, to encourage flowering in summer and autumn. When the flowers die, trim the short stem back to the top of the pseudobulb.

POSITION

Suits a warm room, such as a kitchen or lounge, which does not fall below 12°C (54°C). Keep in a north-facing room and shade from the summer sun to prevent leaves burning, but move into direct sun in winter.

REPOT

These orchids have a long rhizome connecting the pseudobulbs, so can end up creeping over the edge of the pot quite easily. This means they need to be repotted into a larger pot every 2–3 years with coarse orchid bark.

THE RELATIVES

Corsage orchids

Corsage orchids are found throughout South America, and come in all forms, from miniature species to large, blowsy hybrids. Whichever you choose, they all enjoy the same warm conditions.

GUARIANTHE AURANTIACA ▶
Closely related to cattleyas, this orchid from Mexico and Central America boasts dense heads of bright orange flowers.

◀ CATTLEYA BICOLOR
This tall species can reach 60cm (24in) high. Its slender pseudobulbs are surprisingly strong, and produce bold bronze and magenta flowers.

◄ CATTLEYA TRIANAE
*The impressive, frilled,
scented, lavender flowers of
this slow-growing species can
reach up to 20cm (8in) across.*

CATTLEYA FORBESII ►
*More compact than most corsage
orchids, reaching 25cm (10in) tall,
this green-bloomed Brazilian species
is free-flowering and easy to grow.*

◄ CATTLEYA PURPURATA
*This species delivers large heads
of several white, fragrant flowers,
although the colour of the frilly
purple lip varies among its many
natural varieties.*

TOP FIVE
EASY-CARE

Choosing an orchid that's right for you can be a challenge. These varieties are all easy to care for and will make sure you get off to a successful start.

MOTH ORCHID
Phalaenopsis
Cool Breeze

With their long-lasting blooms and ability to thrive in any warm room, moth orchids are all perfect for beginners. This classic, crisp white variety flowers freely all year round, and will add a touch of elegance to any space.

See pp.114–115.

DANCING LADIES
Oncidium
Sweet Sugar

This easy-going hybrid is a must for any cool room, where its gorgeous sprays of bright yellow flowers will add a vivid splash of colour for weeks at a time, and will flower reliably every year when mature.

See pp.98–99.

Pleione formosana

Given a cold room, this dainty little species orchid couldn't be simpler to care for. The rule to remember is: when it has leaves, water it, and when it doesn't, don't. After a few years, large plants produce a fabulous early spring display.

See pp.120–121.

WARM-GROWING SLIPPER ORCHID

Paphiopedilum Maudiae

This exotic appearance of this slipper orchid belies the fact that it is trouble-free to grow, and will do well alongside moth orchids in a warm room. An elegant green flower will emerge once a year from the newest rosette of mottled leaves.

See pp.108–109.

Dendrobium Berry Oda

Encourage this tough Australian orchid to produce its striking sprays of fragrant, pink flowers in spring, simply by keeping it in a cool room and allowing the roots to dry out in winter.

See pp.66–67.

RAG ORCHID

Coelogyne cristata

Mimicking the summer monsoon rains and dry winters of the rag orchid's native range is the key to success. The rag-like frilled edges of these striking, snow-white winter flowers inspired their name

VITAL STATISTICS

HOW IT GROWS This orchid is an epiphyte with a spreading, sympodial habit, which anchors itself to trees with aerial roots.

ORIGIN Native to cool, moist areas in northern India and the Himalayas.

ANATOMY This spreading orchid forms a tight clump of rounded pseudobulbs, which produce dark green leaves, and increase in number annually.

SIZE Leaves reach 20cm (8in) high, with large flowers held among them on 30cm (12in) long stems. In time, clumps spread to 40cm (16in) wide.

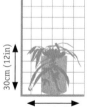

30cm (12in)

40cm (16in)

WATER

In spring, water weekly and continue as the new pseudobulbs grow through summer. Once the pseudobulbs have matured, only water when they start to wrinkle. This species needs a winter rest, so hardly any water is needed for the winter months.

POSITION

Keep cool in summer, with a maximum of 20°C (68°F), and shaded from direct sun: a north-facing room is ideal. Choose a cool, unheated room in winter, where the temperature drops to 10°C (50°F) at night.

HELP TO FLOWER

Plants kept cold and dry during winter will flower well in late winter and early spring, and produce good summer growth. When the flowers have died, trim the dead stems back to the base.

FEED

Use a high-nitrogen fertilizer every 2–3 waterings throughout spring and summer to fuel the new growth. Move to a high-potash fertilizer in late summer and autumn to mature the growth and encourage flowering. No feeding is needed in winter.

REPOT

Move into a larger pot every 2–3 years in summer after flowering, when the new pseudobulbs reach the edge of their current pot. Use medium grade bark chippings. These orchids form large clumps in time, but can be divided up and repotted if too big.

THE RELATIVES

Rag orchids

Orchids from the large Coelogyne family are found across Southeast Asia, in a fascinating array of sizes and flower colours. They all enjoy plentiful moisture while growing followed by a dry period of rest.

COELOGYNE FLACCIDA ▶
An elegant species, found at high altitudes from Nepal to Thailand. Its arching flower stems hold many fragrant, creamy white blooms.

◀ COELOGYNE MASSANGEANA
Long, pendent stems of soft yellow blooms emerge from among large leaves and pseudobulbs, often twice a year. This species prefers slightly warmer conditions.

◄ COELOGYNE MOOREANA
*A beautiful and sought-after
species from Vietnam, with an
upright stem of large, white,
orange-throated flowers.*

COELOGYNE NITIDA ▶
*This delightful spring-flowering
species has sparkling white flowers,
with a yellow-orange lip, which are
extremely sweetly scented.*

◄ COELOGYNE SPECIOSA
*Unusual and attractive, the large,
dark apricot-coloured flowers
of this species are produced in
succession during winter.*

BOAT ORCHID

Cymbidium Castle of Mey 'Pinkie'

Ideal for a cool room, this smaller-flowered boat orchid is a good choice for beginners, with elegant strap-like leaves and tall stems of delicate, shell-pink flowers.

VITAL STATISTICS

HOW IT GROWS
This sympodial orchid can naturally be either epiphytic or terrestrial.

ORIGIN Native to India and Southeast Asia.

ANATOMY Produces tightly packed pseudobulbs and arching, strap-like leaves. Tall, curved flower stems are borne from winter to spring.

SIZE The leaves reach up to 50cm (20in) tall and spread 30cm (12in) wide. The impressive flower stems can be 70cm (28in) high.

70cm (28in)

30cm (12in)

WATER
Water from the top of the pot and drain well. Never stand in water. In spring and summer, water weekly, and every 2–3 weeks in autumn and winter. Let the pot dry between waterings.

POSITION
Keep cool (below 20°C/68°F) and shade from direct sunlight during summer: a north-facing room or shady spot outdoors is ideal. In winter, keep in an unheated room, where the temperature drops to 10°C (50°F) at night.

HELP TO FLOWER

A cool winter will encourage prolific flowering, as will strong summer growth. When the flowers have died, trim the dead stems back to the base of the plant.

FEED

In spring and summer, feed new growth with a high-nitrogen fertilizer every 2–3 waterings. Change to a high-potash fertilizer in late summer and autumn to mature the growth and encourage flowering. Do not feed in winter.

REPOT

Every 2–3 years, or when the pseudobulbs have filled the top of the pot, repot in the spring, once flowering has finished. Use medium or coarse grade bark chippings.

THE RELATIVES

Boat orchids

There are many attractive boat orchid hybrids to choose from, but don't overlook the less commonly grown species, which will also flourish in the same cool growing conditions.

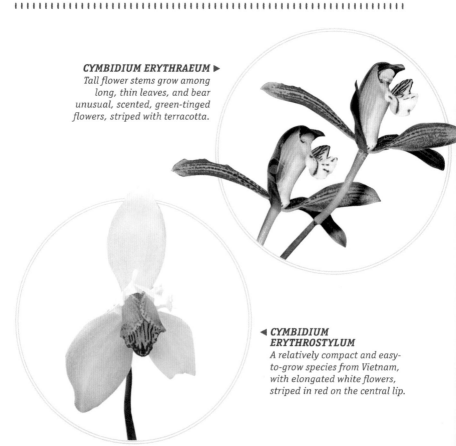

CYMBIDIUM ERYTHRAEUM ▶
Tall flower stems grow among long, thin leaves, and bear unusual, scented, green-tinged flowers, striped with terracotta.

◀ CYMBIDIUM ERYTHROSTYLUM
A relatively compact and easy-to-grow species from Vietnam, with elongated white flowers, striped in red on the central lip.

◄ CYMBIDIUM GOERINGII
*This miniature species, from
Japan, China, and Korea, has
delicate green flowers, and is
known as the noble orchid.*

CYMBIDIUM LOWIANUM ►
*The spectacular yellow-green
flowers of this large species
have a contrasting rust-red lip,
and are produced on stems up
to 1m (39in) tall.*

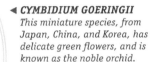

**◄ CYMBIDIUM SARAH JEAN
'ICE CASCADE'**
*Ideal for a hanging basket,
this easy variety produces many
pendent flower stems dripping
with pure white flowers.*

DENDROBIUM SPRING DREAM

Reliable, with stems smothered in scented, white flowers, this is one of many cool-growing dendrobiums. Popular houseplants, they need to be kept away from summer heat.

VITAL STATISTICS

HOW IT GROWS As a sympodial epiphyte, with aerial roots to anchor it to the branch of a tree.

ORIGIN Native to India and Southeast Asia.

ANATOMY Leaves are produced along tall, green, cane-like pseudobulbs, which grow to form a clump. Clusters of flowers bloom along each cane's length.

SIZE Sturdy flowering canes reach up to 60cm (24in) tall, and mature specimens will spread to form stands of flowering canes up to 25cm (10in) across.

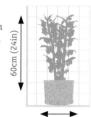

60cm (24in)

25cm (10in)

WATER

Water from the top and drain well. Never stand the pot in water. Water weekly during spring and summer, and every 2–3 weeks in autumn and winter. Allow to dry out between waterings.

POSITION

Keep cool (below 20°C/68°F) during summer and out of direct sunlight to prevent leaf damage: a north-facing room is ideal. In winter, move to a cool, unheated room, where the temperature drops to 10°C (50°F) at night.

HELP TO FLOWER

A cool winter, and good summer growth thanks to careful feeding and watering, will promote flowers every year. When flowers die, trim off their short stems, but do not cut the tall, cane-like pseudobulb.

FEED

Apply a high-nitrogen fertilizer every 2–3 waterings in spring and summer to boost new growth. A high-potash fertilizer in late summer and autumn will mature growth and encourage flowering. Do not feed in winter.

REPOT

Repot in the spring, after flowering, every 2–3 years, or when the tall pseudobulbs have spread to fill the top of the pot. Use medium grade bark chippings.

THE RELATIVES

These other cool-growing *Dendrobium* hybrids thrive in the same conditions, but come in an array of bold colours.

DENDROBIUM COMET KING
Large, scented flowers, in rich magenta-pink with a contrasting white and yellow centre, cluster around each cane.

DENDROBIUM IRENE SMILE
This variety has a striking combination of white flowers with dark pink tips and a pale green centre.

DENDROBIUM POLAR FIRE

This beautiful, compact plant has slender winter stems of long-lasting, white flowers, with magenta-stained centres. It is a warm-growing Dendrobium; ideal for a cosy, bright room.

VITAL STATISTICS

HOW IT GROWS As a sympodial epiphyte, with aerial roots to anchor it to the branch of a tree.

ORIGIN Native to the forests of Southeast Asia.

ANATOMY Upright, thick, cane-like pseudobulbs grow in a clump. Flower sprays emerge from their tips on long, slender stems.

SIZE When in leaf, the canes can reach 20cm (8in) tall. Topped with flower stems, they grow to 50cm (20in) high. Plants spread to 20cm (8in) wide.

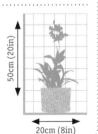

50cm (20in)

20cm (8in)

WATER

Water from the top of the pot and allow to drain well, but never stand in water. Water weekly in spring and summer, and every 2–3 weeks in autumn and winter. Always allow the roots to dry out well in between waterings.

POSITION

Thrives in a warm room, such as a kitchen, which has a maximum of 25°C (77°F) and doesn't fall below 15°C (59°F) at night. Shade the leaves in summer, but move into direct sunlight in winter.

HELP TO FLOWER

Warmth and good light encourage a spray of flowers from the tip of the newest pseudobulb when it matures. When the flowers fade, trim the dead stems back to the cane, but do not cut off the tall, cane-like pseudobulb.

FEED

When plants are in growth during spring and summer, use a high-nitrogen fertilizer every 2–3 waterings. Change to a high-potash fertilizer in late summer and autumn to mature growth and encourage flowering. Do not feed in winter.

REPOT

Repot every 2–3 years in spring, after flowering, once the upright pseudobulbs have spread to fill the top of the pot. Use medium grade bark chippings.

THE RELATIVES

Dendrobium hybrids that flourish in warm conditions produce long-lasting blooms in a wide range of colours.

DENDROBIUM SA-NOOK BLUE HAPPINESS
The unusual deep purplish-blue hue of these flowers is striking and contrasts beautifully with the pale buds.

DENDROBIUM EMMA GOLD
Long stems are laden with flowers in an eye-catching combination of yellow-green and burgundy, which last well when cut.

DENDROBIUM BERRY ODA

Kept cool and well-drained, this tough Australian Dendrobium will reward beginners with plentiful pink, fragrant flowers in late winter and spring.

VITAL STATISTICS

HOW IT GROWS As an epiphyte with a spreading, sympodial habit, and aerial roots to anchor it to the branch of a tree.

ORIGIN Native to open forests in eastern Australia.

ANATOMY Forms clumps of upright, thin pseudobulbs, which produce several leaves along their length, and a spray of flowers at their tip.

SIZE The pseudobulbs and leaves can reach a height of 40cm (16in), increasing to 50cm (20in) when topped with flowering stems. Mature plants spread to 25cm (10in).

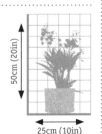

50cm (20in)

25cm (10in)

WATER

Water from the top of the pot, allow to drain well, and never stand the pot in water. Always let roots dry out between waterings. Water weekly in spring and summer, and every 2–3 weeks in autumn and winter.

POSITION

In summer, place in a north-facing room to keep plants as cool as possible and the delicate leaves shaded from direct sunlight. Transfer to a cool, unheated room in winter, where the temperature drops to 10°C (50°F) at night.

HELP TO FLOWER

A period of cool in winter, and strong growth during summer, will both promote repeat flowering. When the flowers die, trim their stems back to the cane, but take care not to cut off the tall, slim pseudobulb.

FEED

A high-nitrogen fertilizer every 2–3 waterings will boost the new growth throughout spring and summer. Use a high-potash fertilizer in late summer and autumn to mature the growth and encourage flowering. No feeding is needed in winter.

REPOT

Repot in the spring, after flowering, every 2–3 years, or when the tall pseudobulbs have filled the top of the pot. Use medium grade bark chippings.

THE RELATIVES

Other fascinating Australian species of *Dendrobium* will thrive in the same conditions.

DENDROBIUM KINGIANUM
Robust and vigorous, this delightful species also produces small, bright pink blooms with a delicate scent.

DENDROBIUM SPECIOSUM
Given ample space, this magnificent species reaches 90cm (36in) tall and has spectacular sprays of many small, scented, yellow flowers.

PINEAPPLE ORCHID

Dendrobium densiflorum

Grow this spectacular orchid in a hanging basket to best appreciate its huge, pendent sprays of bright yellow flowers in spring. Like many other Dendrobium species, it is surprisingly simple to grow successfully.

VITAL STATISTICS

HOW IT GROWS As an epiphyte with a spreading, sympodial habit, and aerial roots to anchor it to the branch of a tree.

ORIGIN Native to Nepal, Malaysia, and China.

ANATOMY The upright, tall pseudobulbs grow in a clump, and produce lance-shaped leaves, and pendent flower stems.

SIZE Pseudobulbs with leaves at their tips grow up to 50cm (20in) tall. The large, pendent flower spray can reach 26cm (10in) long.

50cm (20in)

20cm (8in)

WATER

Water from the top of the pot and drain. Never allow to stand in water. Water weekly in spring and summer, and every 2–3 weeks in autumn and winter. Let the roots dry out in between waterings.

POSITION

Ideally, place in a north-facing room for summer, where plants can be kept below 20°C (68°F) and out of direct sunlight. Move to a cool, unheated room in winter, where the temperature drops to 10°C (50°F) at night.

HELP TO FLOWER

Given a cool winter rest and plenty of water to produce good summer growth, this orchid should flower reliably. When the flowers have died, trim the stems back to the cane, taking care not cut off the tall, narrow pseudobulb.

FEED

Do not feed during the winter rest, but apply a high-nitrogen fertilizer every 2–3 waterings throughout spring and summer, when in growth. Use a high-potash fertilizer in late summer and autumn to mature the growth and encourage flowering.

REPOT

Repot in the spring, after flowering, every 2–3 years, or when the tall pseudobulbs have filled the top of the pot. Use medium grade bark chippings.

THE RELATIVES

Dendrobium is a vast genus of orchids. These easy-to-grow species thrive in the same conditions as *D. densiflorum*.

DENDROBIUM INFUNDIBULUM
Large and long-lasting, these translucent white flowers, with an orange throat, are produced at the tips of tall, slender canes.

DENDROBIUM WILLIAMSONII
A more compact species with short, stocky canes and a cluster of several highly scented, cream or yellow flowers.

TOP FIVE
WEIRD AND WONDERFUL

The orchid family boasts some of the most extraordinary flowers in the plant kingdom. These strange species are bound to create a talking point when they bloom in your home.

1

TULIP ORCHID
Anguloa clowesii

This statuesque orchid can reach 80cm (32in) tall, and produces hard, waxy, tulip-like blooms, which have an unreal look about them, and attract pollinating insects with their extraordinary medicinal scent.

See pp.36–37.

2

SPIDER ORCHID
Brassia Orange Delight

The thin, long-petalled flowers of Brassia orchids are said to resemble exotic spiders and always make a spectacular show. With elegant, arching stems of spotted, orange flowers, B. Orange Delight is no exception.

See pp.42–43.

3

UPSIDE-DOWN ORCHID
Stanhopea tigrina

*Everything about stanhopeas is peculiar!
Their flower stems grow downwards, producing
short-lived waxy blooms that are amazing to
touch, and will fill a room with their heady scent.*

See pp.132–133.

4

Bulbophyllum lobbii

*Bulbophyllums are some
of the weirdest of all
orchids, and B. lobbii is
no exception. Its large
flowers are borne singly
at the end of long stems,
where sculpted, swept
back petals surround a
curious rocking lip at
their centre.*

See p.44–45.

5

Restrepia cuprea

*A true miniature orchid, this species has exquisite
boat-shaped flowers with copper-orange colouring,
which are best viewed through a magnifying glass.
These diminutive treasures are ideal for terrariums
(see p.107) or where space is limited.*

See pp.130–131.

CHAIN ORCHID

Dendrochilum glumaceum

Care is needed to water and feed this winter-growing orchid correctly, but the reward is graceful, arching stems packed with sweetly scented, white winter blooms.

VITAL STATISTICS

HOW IT GROWS As a sympodial epiphyte, with aerial roots to anchor it securely to a tree branch or trunk.

ORIGIN Native to Borneo and the Philippines.

ANATOMY Produces small, rounded pseudobulbs with long, broad leaves, which form a clump over time. Flower stems are produced from new growth.

SIZE Large leaves can reach 30cm (12in) tall, and spread into a clump about 20cm across. The magnificent arching flower stems are up to 40cm (16in) long.

30cm (12in)

20cm (8in)

WATER

Allow to dry out between waterings, but check weekly and water once the roots are dry. Always water from the top of the pot and allow to drain well, never standing the pot in water.

POSITION

Find this orchid a light position, out of bright summer sun, in a room of intermediate temperature, above 12°C (54°F). Try a kitchen or bathroom, where it is easy to spray regularly to increase humidity.

HELP TO FLOWER

Encourage this orchid into bloom by keeping the plant correctly fed and regularly watered during its winter growth. Once flowers have faded, trim their dead stems back to the base.

FEED

This orchid grows in the winter and rests in summer, so use a high-nitrogen fertilizer in the winter growing season, and a high-potash fertilizer when the new pseudobulbs are swelling as growth ends in spring.

REPOT

Repot every 2–3 years or when the existing pot is full of pseudobulbs. Use medium or coarse grade bark chippings. Large specimens can be divided in spring, after flowering.

THE RELATIVES

All chain orchids produce spectacular pendent or arching sprays of winter flowers and make great specimen plants.

DENDROCHILUM COBBIANUM
Compact and elegant, with long, arching, chain-like stems of fragrant, creamy yellow flowers in winter.

DENDROCHILUM WENZELLII
A shorter species with thick, grass-like leaves but no pseudobulb. The dramatic, spiky stems of flowers are an unusual bright red.

TABLE MOUNTAIN ORCHID

Disa uniflora

The bright orange, geometric, spring and summer flowers of this sought-after species make it well worth the effort of perfecting its unusual wet conditions.

VITAL STATISTICS

HOW IT GROWS As a terrestrial orchid, with a sympodial habit. It is found growing in damp soil and streams.

ORIGIN Native to the Cape Provinces of South Africa.

ANATOMY New shoots grow from an underground tuber, forming rosettes of leaves from which flower stems grow.

SIZE The lance-shaped leaves grow up to 10cm (4in) high, and spread 20cm (8in) wide, while the flower stems can reach 50cm (20in) tall.

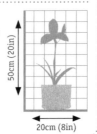

50cm (20in)

20cm (8in)

WATER

As a native of damp soils and streams, this orchid prefers to stand in a tray of rainwater at all times. The water should be changed every week to keep the plant healthy.

POSITION

Keep plants in a shady, well-ventilated spot in summer, below 24°C (75°F), and move to a very cool place in winter, with night-time temperatures below 10°C (50°F). Try a windowsill in a cold room, or a greenhouse with some frost protection.

HELP TO FLOWER

Ensuring that the roots are kept continually moist during the growing season, and that plants are exposed to cool winter temperatures, encourages new flowers every year.

FEED

Add a weak high-nitrogen fertilizer (half usual dilution rate) into the water in the tray once a week during spring and autumn. Do not apply fertilizer through the pot.

REPOT

Repot every 1–2 years, in early spring, as new rosettes of leaves begin to grow, using a mix of peat and perlite.

THE RELATIVES

The bright neon colours of *Disa* make them irresistible to any orchid collector, and there is an amazing array to choose from.

DISA DIORES
A brilliant orange-red hybrid, which sometimes also has flowers in shades of electric pink.

DISA KEWENSIS
The smaller flowers of this extremely showy variety are usually yellow and often have attractive orange markings.

DRACULA BELLA

Ideal for hanging baskets, these curious, spotted, triangular flowers, with their 20cm (8in) long tails, hang below the plant on delicate stems. They flourish in cool, moist conditions similar to those found in their native cloud forests.

VITAL STATISTICS

HOW IT GROWS This orchid is an epiphyte, with a spreading, sympodial habit. It is found growing in the branches of trees.

ORIGIN Native to high-altitude Colombian cloud forests.

ANATOMY These orchids have no pseudobulbs, and instead produce narrow leaves in a clump, and thin flower stems that hang downwards.

SIZE Foliage reaches 20cm (8in) in height, and clusters of leaves spread to 20cm (8in) wide. The slender flower stems can be 20cm (8in) long.

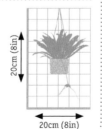

20cm (8in)

20cm (8in)

WATER

This orchid thrives when its roots are kept moist, so add absorbent sphagnum moss to the potting mix, and check the pot weekly. Water from above and do not leave the plant standing in water.

POSITION

Choose a cool, shady, well-ventilated place, 10–20°C (50–68°F), where moisture can easily be maintained around the roots. Hanging baskets are ideal, because flowers emerge from the base of the plant, even through the basket, on pendent stems.

REPOT

Repot every 2–3 years, or when the new leaves have filled the existing pot or basket, using a moisture-retentive mix of sphagnum moss and perlite.

HELP TO FLOWER

Keep plants moist and cool to encourage flowering from winter to summer. After the first flower has dropped, the same stem may make more buds, so leave it until it has gone brown and died.

FEED

Add a little high-nitrogen fertilizer every 2–3 waterings in the spring and summer, then change to a high-potash fertilizer in the late summer and autumn. Be careful not to overfeed, as a build up of salts around the roots can be damaging.

THE RELATIVES

The weird flowers of *Dracula* were likened to dragon's mouths, inspiring their Latin name, which means "dragon".

DRACULA SIMIA
Known as the monkey orchid, the smaller flowers of this more compact species really do strongly resemble a monkey's face.

DRACULA VAMPIRA
Fascinating and slightly sinister, these are the genus' darkest flowers, with large, long-tailed blooms, heavily veined in black.

CRUCIFIX ORCHID

Epidendrum radicans

Known as the crucifix orchid due to its cross-shaped lip, this substantial orchid requires plenty of room to flourish: a corner in a cool conservatory would provide an ideal space.

VITAL STATISTICS

HOW IT GROWS This orchid has a spreading, sympodial habit, and grows as a terrestrial in grassland and on roadsides.

ORIGIN Native to the tropical Americas.

ANATOMY Forms tall, cane-like stems with short, thick leaves along their length. Flower stems emerge from the top of these main stems, between the leaves.

SIZE With clusters of flowers at their tips, stems can reach a huge 130cm (51in) tall, but thanks to their small leaves, only spread to 30cm (12in).

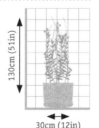

130cm (51in)

30cm (12in)

WATER

Water from the top of the pot and drain well. Do not stand the pot in water. Always allow time for the pot to dry out and check that it has before the next watering. Water weekly in spring and summer, and every 2–3 weeks in autumn and winter. Mist the leaves daily.

POSITION

Provide a cool room with a minimum temperature of 10°C (50°F) in winter, and a bright spot out of direct sun in summer, with a maximum of 20°C (68°F). Try a cool conservatory in winter and moving outdoors during summer.

HELP TO FLOWER

A cooler winter and lots of light will both encourage re-flowering. Given the correct treatment this orchid should flower happily each year, from the top of the matured stem. When the flowers have finished, trim off their dead stems back to the leaves.

FEED

Use a high-nitrogen fertilizer every 2–3 waterings during the growing season, when new leaves and stems are being formed. Use a high-potash fertilizer when the stem has reached its full height to encourage flowering.

REPOT

Repot when the increased size and height of the plant has made it top heavy and a larger pot will give it more stability. This is usually necessary every 2–3 years, or more often if it is growing well. Use medium or coarse bark chippings.

THE RELATIVES

Epidendrums come in all sizes; from giants to tiny miniatures. These examples enjoy the same conditions as *E. radicans*.

EPIDENDRUM PORPAX
A miniature, 5cm (2.5in) tall, with a creeping habit. Its relatively large green flowers have a glossy red lip.

***EPICATTLEYA* RENÉ MARQUÉS**
This popular old hybrid has a tall, reed-like habit. Its multi-coloured, waxy flowers cascade from cane-tops on slim stems.

LAELIA ANCEPS

Easy and elegant, this Laelia just needs simple care and plenty of space for its tall winter blooms. It often grows into a large specimen, but is easily divided into smaller plants.

VITAL STATISTICS

HOW IT GROWS As a sympodial epiphyte on the branches of trees, with thick aerial roots to anchor it.

ORIGIN From Mexico, Guatemala, and Honduras.

ANATOMY Elongated, oval-shaped pseudobulbs each produce 1–2 thick, leathery leaves, and flower stems at their tips.

SIZE Leaves reach a height and spread of 20cm (8in). The long, slender flower stems grow up to 70cm (28in) tall.

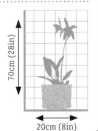

70cm (28in)

20cm (8in)

WATER

Water from the top of the pot and allow to drain well. Do not stand in water. Allow to dry out well between waterings. Water weekly, and mist regularly, in spring and summer and water every 2–3 weeks in autumn and winter.

POSITION

Find a spot in a room with an intermediate temperature range (12–25°C/54–77°F). Keep the delicate leaves shaded from the summer sun. A place by a north-facing window is ideal for summer, moving into direct light for winter.

HELP TO FLOWER

Good light, and a dry winter rest, will help to encourage the growth of a strong new pseudobulb and reliable flowering each year. Staking may be required to support the tall flower stems. When the flowers die, trim the stem back to the top of the pseudobulb.

FEED

Use a high-nitrogen fertilizer every 2–3 waterings in spring and summer to boost the new growth. Switch to a high-potash fertilizer in late summer and autumn, to mature the growth, and encourage flowering. No feeding is required in winter.

REPOT

A long rhizome connects the pseudobulbs, which allows plants to creep over the edge of the pot quite rapidly. This means they need to be repotted every 2–3 years, into a larger pot containing coarse bark chippings.

THE RELATIVES

These showy *Laelia* species flourish given plenty of light, a drier spell in winter, and high humidity during summer.

LAELIA GOULDIANA
This native of Mexico has large, long-lasting, purple-pink flowers on a tall stem, which make an impressive show.

LAELIA AUTUMNALIS
Several dramatic, deep pink blooms are held high on stems up to 100cm (40in) tall, during late autumn.

JEWEL ORCHID

Ludisia discolor

Although this orchid has pretty white flowers, it is also prized for its attractive red-striped leaves, which sparkle like a jewel when you shine a light on them in the dark.

VITAL STATISTICS

HOW IT GROWS This is a terrestrial orchid, found growing in damp, shady conditions. It has a spreading, sympodial habit.

ORIGIN Native to rainforest in Southeast Asia.

ANATOMY Long, spreading rhizomes form between leaf shoots, but produce no pseudobulbs. Flower stems arise from the centre of leaf rosettes.

SIZE The foliage of these small plants reaches only 15cm (6in) high. The flower stems can be up to 40cm (16in) tall.

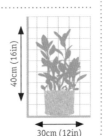

40cm (16in)

30cm (12in)

WATER

These orchids like to be damp, so check, and water from the top of the pot as soon as there are signs the compost is drying out. Allow to drain well, and do not stand in water. Avoid splashing the leaves, and wipe off any drops of water.

POSITION

Place in a warm room with a minimum of 18°C (64°F) in winter, and a maximum of 25°C (77°F) in summer, when the soft leaves also need shade. The humidity in a warm kitchen or bathroom could be ideal.

HELP TO FLOWER

Warm, humid conditions will encourage the production of new leaf rosettes, each of which should form a flowering stem once matured. After flowering, trim the dead stem back to the leaves. Use a thin stake to support the tall flower stem.

FEED

Use a high-nitrogen fertilizer every 2–3 waterings when the new leaves are growing. Use a high-potash fertilizer when the new rosette of leaves is maturing to encourage the plant into flowering.

REPOT

Repot when the plant has increased in size to reach the edge of the pot. This is usually necessary every 2–3 years or more often if it grows well. Wait until after flowering when the new leaf shoot starts to grow. Use a peat and perlite mix, or similar, with houseplant compost, not bark chips.

LYCASTE AROMATICA

In spring and early summer, this free-flowering species produces multiple, sweetly scented flowers around the base of the plant. Naturally deciduous, this orchid needs a winter rest somewhere cool.

VITAL STATISTICS

HOW IT GROWS
A sympodial orchid, usually found in damp ground as a terrestrial, but occasionally as an epiphyte.

ORIGIN
Native to Central America.

ANATOMY
A cluster of oval pseudobulbs forms tall, broad, deciduous leaves. Multiple single flowers arise from the base.

SIZE
Leaves reach 25cm (10in) tall, with the shorter flower stems growing up to 15cm (6in) high. In time plants spread to 20cm (8in) wide.

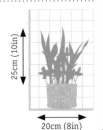

25cm (10in)

20cm (8in)

WATER
Water new growth weekly through spring and summer. Leaves should also be misted daily during summer. Once the leaves drop, stop watering unless the pseudobulbs start to wrinkle. Do not water in winter, to allow plants a period of dry winter rest.

POSITION
In winter, choose a cool, unheated room where the temperature drops to 10°C (50°F) at night. Keep as cool as possible in summer, with a maximum of 20°C (68°F), and shade the soft leaves from damaging bright summer sunlight.

HELP TO FLOWER

A winter rest and strong summer growth both encourage good blooms. When the flowers have died, trim the dead stems back to the base of the plant.

FEED

Use a high-nitrogen feed every 2–3 waterings in spring and summer to fuel new growth. A high-potash feed in late summer and autumn encourages flowering. No feeding is required in winter.

THE RELATIVES

These *Lycaste* species thrive in the same conditions, and produce triangular blooms from the base of the plant.

LYCASTE VIRGINALIS
Found from southern Mexico to Honduras, these large, waxy flowers can be white or blushed shades of pale or deep pink.

LYCASTE DEPPEI
Numerous green and brown, short-stemmed flowers cluster at the base of this Central American species.

REPOT

Repot every 1–2 years in summer after flowering, when the pseudobulbs have filled the pot. Use a mix of fine bark, perlite, and sphagnum moss, or similar.

KITE ORCHID

Masdevallia coccinea

Tall, thin stems with bright flowers waving at the tip look just like kites flying in the wind, and will be produced every year given the cool, humid conditions they love.

VITAL STATISTICS

HOW IT GROWS This orchid has a sympodial habit, and grows as an epiphyte on the branches of trees at high altitudes.

ORIGIN Native to the cloud forests of Colombia.

ANATOMY Narrow leaves form a clump, with no pseudobulbs. The thin flower stems grow upwards, each producing a single bloom.

SIZE The slender leaves reach 25cm (10in) long, and plants spread to 15cm (6in) wide, with 40cm (16in) flower stems arching above them.

40cm (16in)

15cm (6in)

WATER

Keep the roots moist at all times; they do best in sphagnum moss, which helps retain moisture. Check the pot weekly and, when drying out, water from above. Do not stand in water. Mist leaves regularly to create humidity.

POSITION

Choose a cool, shady, well-ventilated spot, with a temperature range of 10–20°C (50–68°F). Ensure that they don't get too hot in summer. They like the air movement created by a fan.

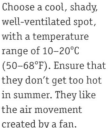

HELP TO FLOWER

A strong plant grown in cool, moist conditions should re-flower easily, although the season in which it flowers can naturally vary. After flowers have died, trim the dead stem to the base. Flower stems may need a thin stake.

FEED

During spring and summer, add a high-nitrogen fertilizer every 2–3 waterings, then a high-potash feed in late summer and autumn.

REPOT

Repot every 2–3 years or when the new leaves have filled the pot. Use a mix of sphagnum moss and perlite.

THE RELATIVES

Other species and hybrids of *Masdevallia* need the same growing conditions, and most make compact plants.

MASDEVALLIA BARLAEANA
A bright red species, with several flower stems at a time held above the clump-forming foliage.

MASDEVALLIA CORIACEA
Olive-green flowers with dark purple stripes are produced on shorter stems around the base of the plant.

TOP FIVE

BEAUTIFULLY SIMPLE DISPLAY IDEAS

The natural elegance of an orchid is often its greatest charm. These simple ways to display orchids add a little style and originality, without detracting from their fabulous blooms.

DECORATIVE POTS

Instantly enhance the appearance of orchids growing in plastic pots by placing them into decorative containers. Plain or patterned, and made from a variety of materials, these "cover pots" should ideally have a dome or ridge in their base to prevent the plastic pot standing in water. Attractive perforated clay pots are good for drainage and can be used as cover pots or planted into directly.

Try with dancing ladies, see pp.98–99.

Twisted willow twigs make stylish stakes

Perforated pots allow light in to roots and aid drainage

STAKING

Support the stems of large-flowered orchids to prevent them breaking, and to add an extra element to the display. Use simple bamboo or split green canes, or get creative with coloured supports or twisted willow twigs. Train stems in natural arches, or even into shapes like a cascade or a heart.

Try with moth orchids, see pp.114–115.

GROWING IN A VASE

An elegant glass vase makes a great display case, and creates a perfect warm, humid microclimate, where orchids can thrive. Place any orchid in a pot in a suitably sized vase and remove it to water. The dramatic aerial roots of vandas look spectacular curled directly into a vase.

Try with *Vanda* Blue Magic, see pp.136–137.

A large vase can also hold foliage and flowers

MOUNTING

The most naturalistic way to grow epiphytic orchids is to mount them onto pieces of cork bark, fern fibre, or even branches, with some moss to retain moisture around their roots. Regular misting and dunking are essential to keep humidity high, but this rainforest look is worth the effort.

Try mounting orchids with a creeping habit, such as *Dendrobium* Berry Oda, see pp.66–67.

Attach chains to a colander for a hanging basket

CREATIVE CONTAINERS

Orchids will grow in almost any container, provided that it has plenty of drainage holes, so let your imagination run wild, and create your own quirky orchid pots. Sieves, colanders, or old baskets are ideal, but with a little ingenuity, stylish containers can be created from almost anything.

Try with spider orchids, see pp.42–43.

MAXILLARIA PRAESTANS

The colourful, winged, triangular flowers shooting up from the base of this robust plant are typical of the Maxillaria family. This undemanding species is the perfect choice for beginners.

VITAL STATISTICS

HOW IT GROWS This orchid has a sympodial habit and is found as an epiphyte on tree branches, with aerial roots to anchor it.

ORIGIN Native to humid forests in Central America.

ANATOMY Forms oval-shaped pseudobulbs, each with a thick, leathery leaf at its tip, and a flower stem from its base.

SIZE Plants can reach up to 30cm (12in) tall, and spread to a width of 40cm (16in). Their flower stems grow to 15cm (6in) high.

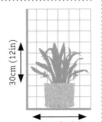

30cm (12in)

40cm (16in)

WATER

Water from the top of the pot and drain well. Do not stand in water. Allow to dry out thoroughly between waterings. Water weekly in spring and summer and every 2–3 weeks in autumn and winter. Mist the leaves daily for extra humidity.

POSITION

Locate in a room with an intermediate temperature: a minimum of 12°C (54°F) in winter and a maximum 20°C (68°F). Provide good, bright, but indirect sunlight in summer. A humid bathroom or kitchen window may suit, where leaves can be misted regularly.

"Provide good, bright, but indirect sunlight in summer and mist the leaves daily for extra humidity."

HELP TO FLOWER

Good light, humidity, and a strong new pseudobulb, will all encourage re-flowering. Given the correct treatment, this orchid should flower happily, alongside its new leaf shoots, each year. When the flowers are over, trim the dead stems back to the base of the plant.

FEED

Throughout the growing season, when new leaves and bulbs are forming, apply a high-nitrogen fertilizer every 2–3 waterings. Use a high-potash fertilizer when the growth is maturing, to promote flowering.

REPOT

Repot when the growth of new pseudobulbs has reached the edge of the pot. This is usually necessary every 2–3 years, or more often if it grows well. Wait until after flowering, when the plant is producing new leaves, and use medium or coarse bark chippings.

THE RELATIVES

Maxillaria

The extraordinary flowers of these Maxillaria species look impossibly exotic, but in reality they are quite easy to keep, and will bloom repeatedly given good humidity and light.

MAXILLARIA COCCINEA ▶
Clusters of small, bright red flowers are launched from this plant's base on short stems, so that they open among the leaves like fireworks.

◀ MAXILLARIA MELEAGRIS
A small, clump-forming species, with long, thin leaves, and dark-lipped, dusky pink flowers that emerge from the base on short stems.

◄ MAXILLARIA PICTA
*Triangular yellow flowers, marked
with dark red spots, are sweetly
scented, and produced from the
base of this compact plant.*

MAXILLARIA TENUIFOLIA ►
*This species has grassy leaves,
and an upright, climbing habit.
Its orange-red flowers are
distinctly coconut-scented.*

◄ MAXILLARIA VARIABILIS
*The vivid yellow blooms of this
compact, free-flowering species,
nestle among the leaves and
small rounded pseudobulbs,
giving off a curry-like scent.*

MILTONIA SUNSET

with their dazzling shades of yellow and pink, these flowers are reminiscent of a tropical sunset. Although similar to the "pansy orchid" Miltoniopsis, this orchid is a little easier to grow.

VITAL STATISTICS

HOW IT GROWS As a sympodial epiphyte on tree branches, with aerial roots to anchor it.

ORIGIN A native of forests in Brazil.

ANATOMY Forms flattened, oval pseudobulbs, and soft, pale leaves. Flower stems grow from the side of pseudobulbs.

SIZE Leaves reach 30cm (12in) tall, with flowers stems up to 50cm (20in) high. Plants spread to 20cm (8in) wide.

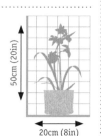

50cm (20in)

20cm (8in)

WATER

These orchids can be prone to overwatering and root rot, so allow to dry out well in between waterings. Check weekly, but only water when the pot is dry. The best way to give the plant moisture is to mist the leaves daily to create humidity, rather than overwater the roots.

POSITION

Place this orchid in a room with an intermediate temperature, ranging from a winter minimum of 12°C (54°C), to a maximum of 20°C (68°F) in summer, when the pale leaves need shade from direct sunlight. Try a humid bathroom or kitchen, where it's easy to mist daily.

HELP TO FLOWER

Given the correct watering, feeding, temperature, and humidity, this orchid should produce good-sized new pseudobulbs each year, from which flower stems will emerge once they are mature. When the flowers have faded, trim off the dead stems. Short stakes help to support the large flowers.

FEED

Use a high-nitrogen fertilizer every 2–3 waterings, when new leaves are growing. Switch to a high-potash fertilizer, as the new pseudobulb is maturing, to promote flowering.

REPOT

It's time to repot when the new pseudobulbs have reached the edge of the pot. This is usually necessary every 2–3 years, or more often if your plant is thriving. Repot after flowering, when a new leaf shoot emerges, using medium or coarse bark chippings.

THE RELATIVES

These *Miltonia* species also have spectacular blooms, and thrive quite easily in the same humid conditions.

MILTONIA SPECTABILIS
With a low, creeping habit, this Brazilian species holds its large lavender and white flowers close to its leaves.

MILTONIA FLAVESCENS
The elegant, star-shaped, soft lemon-yellow flowers of this species burst from buds on upright flower stems.

PANSY ORCHID

Miltoniopsis Herralexandre

These large-flowered orchids are incredibly showy and look just like an overgrown pansy. Careful cultivation, mimicking their humid native habitat, is necessary to coax them into bloom.

VITAL STATISTICS

HOW IT GROWS As a sympodial epiphyte on tree branches, with aerial roots to anchor it.

ORIGIN Native to the mountains of Colombia.

ANATOMY Produces flattened, oval pseudobulbs and soft, pale-green leaves. The flower stem grows from the side of the matured bulb.

SIZE Flower stems can grow to 45cm (18in) high, while the foliage has a height and spread of 30cm (12in).

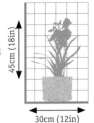

45cm (18in)

30cm (12in)

WATER

Water from the top of the pot, drain well, and do not stand in water. Overwatering these orchids causes root rot, so check weekly, and only water when the pot is dry. Give the plant moisture by misting the leaves daily to create humidity, rather than watering too much at the roots.

POSITION

A place in a humid bathroom or kitchen may suit, where leaves can easily be misted. Provide summer shade to prevent the pale leaves burning, and an intermediate range of temperature: from a winter low of 12°C (54°F) to a summer high of 20°C (68°F).

HELP TO FLOWER

Keeping humidity high and roots fairly dry will help grow good-sized pseudobulbs each year, which will then produce flowers, usually in summer. Trim off the stems of spent flowers. Use short stakes to support the large flowers.

FEED

As the new leaves are growing, use a high-nitrogen fertilizer every 2–3 waterings. Use a high-potash fertilizer when the new pseudobulb is maturing to aid further flowering.

REPOT

Repot when new pseudobulbs have reached the edge of the pot. Do this after flowering, as the new leaf shoot emerges. Repotting is usually needed every 2–3 years. Use medium or coarse bark chippings.

THE RELATIVES

All pansy orchid hybrids like high humidity and their roots kept on the drier side.

MILTONIOPSIS **RED TIDE**
Large, soft, velvety flowers in deep burgundy-red, make a bold display.

MILTONIOPSIS **PINK CADILLAC**
A beautiful bright-pink variety, which is free-flowering when grown well.

DANCING LADIES

Oncidium Sweet Sugar

Showers of vibrant yellow flowers, which resemble the swirling skirts of dancers, are held aloft on tall, graceful stems and make a bold impact in any warm, bright room.

VITAL STATISTICS

HOW IT GROWS This orchid has a sympodial habit and grows as an epiphyte on tree branches, with strong aerial roots to anchor it.

ORIGIN Native to Central and South America.

ANATOMY Each large, oval-shaped pseudobulb produces a pair of broad, dark-green leaves from the top and a tall flower stem from the side.

SIZE Rosettes of leaves reach a height and spread of 20cm (8in), with branched flower stems up to 50cm (20in) tall.

50cm (20in)

20cm (8in)

WATER

Water from the top of the pot, allow to drain, and do not stand in water. Allow to dry out well in between waterings. Water weekly in spring and summer and every 2–3 weeks in autumn and winter. Mist the leaves daily for humidity.

POSITION

Find this orchid a spot with an intermediate temperature range, from a minimum of 12°C (54°F) in winter, to a maximum of 20°C (68°F) in summer, in good, but indirect sunlight. Try a humid bathroom or kitchen, where leaves can be misted regularly.

HELP TO FLOWER

Good light, humidity, and a strong new pseudobulb will encourage re-flowering, so given the correct feeding and watering, this orchid should flower happily each year. When the flowers fade, trim dead stems back to the base of the plant. Tall stems may need supporting stakes.

FEED

Use a high-nitrogen fertilizer every 2–3 waterings throughout the growing season when new leaves and pseudobulbs are being formed. Use a high-potash fertilizer when the growth is maturing to encourage further flowering.

REPOT

It is time to repot when the new pseudobulbs reach the edge of the pot, which is usually every 2–3 years. Repot after flowering, when the new leaf shoot emerges. Use medium or coarse bark chippings.

THE RELATIVES

THE RELATIVES

Oncidium

Many fabulous Oncidium species and hybrids are easy to grow at home, given a little warmth and humidity. The miniatures are ideal for a terrarium, or simply where space is limited.

IIIIIIIIIIIIIIIIIIIIIIIIIIIIIIIIIIIIIIIIIIIIIIIIIIIIIIIIIIIIIIIIIIII

ONCIDIUM CHEIROPHORUM ▶
This miniature species from Central America and Colombia has tiny, strongly scented, bright yellow flowers.

◀ **ONCIDIUM ORNITHORHYNCHUM**
An easy-to-grow miniature species from Colombia and Peru, which produces pretty sprays of fragrant pink flowers in summer.

◄ *ONCIDIUM* **SHARRY BABY**
The branching flower stems of this
showy hybrid reach 80cm (32in)
tall, and bear many deep red,
chocolate-scented flowers.

ONCIDIUM **TWINKLE** ►
Trouble-free to grow and free-
flowering, this cute miniature
hybrid forms dainty sprays of
scented, pink or white blooms.

◄ *ONCIDIUM* **UNGUICULATUM**
The flower stems of this impressive
species from Southern Mexico are laden
with striking yellow and brown blooms,
and can reach 1.5m (5ft) tall.

CAMBRIA ORCHID

Oncidopsis Nelly Isler

Brilliant-scarlet flowers make this variety a must for any beginner's collection. It flourishes given a shady, humid position, and the intensely fragrant blooms will fill a room with scent.

VITAL STATISTICS

HOW IT GROWS This is an epiphyte, with a sympodial habit. It grows on tree branches, with strong aerial roots to anchor it.

ORIGIN From Central and South America.

ANATOMY Each oval-shaped pseudobulb produces a pair of broad, dark-green leaves from the top, and a long flower stem from the side.

SIZE Long leaves grow to 30cm (12in) high, but are dwarfed by the flower stems which reach 50cm (20in) tall. The plant spreads to 20cm (8in).

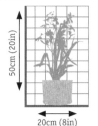

50cm (20in)

20cm (8in)

WATER

Water from the top of the pot and drain well, never standing the pot in water. Allow the pot to dry out in between waterings. Water weekly in spring and summer, and every 2–3 weeks in autumn and winter. Mist the leaves daily to increase humidity levels.

POSITION

Choose a room with an intermediate temperature range: a winter minimum of 12°C (54°F) and a summer maximum of 20°C (68°F) in shade. Try a humid bathroom or kitchen window, where the leaves can be misted regularly.

HELP TO FLOWER

Cooler winter temperatures vand a strong new pseudobulb will promote re-flowering, so given the correct watering and feeding, this orchid should flower happily each year on the matured bulb. When the flowers are over, trim the dead stems back to the base of the plant.

FEED

Use a high-nitrogen fertilizer every 2–3 waterings throughout the growing season, when new leaves and bulbs are being formed. Use a high-potash fertilizer when the growth is maturing to encourage further flowering.

REPOT

It's time to repot when the new pseudobulbs reach the edge of the pot. This is usually necessary every 2–3 years, or more often if the orchid grows really well. Wait until after flowering, when the new leaf shoot starts to grow. Use medium or coarse bark chippings.

THE RELATIVES

Oncidium hybrids

Crossing oncidiums with related orchids has produced a spectacular range of elegant plants, with diverse flower shapes, sizes, and colours. They all thrive easily in the same damp, humid conditions as Oncidopsis Nelly Isler.

**ALICEARA PEGGY ▶
RUTH CARPENTER**
*Arching stems bear several
pointed, spidery, pale pink
flowers, marked with dramatic
deep purple spots.*

**◀ ALICEARA
TAHOMA GLACIER**
*A magnificent orchid, with long
sprays of large, star-shaped,
ice green flowers, blotched
with dusky pink.*

◄ *ONCIDIUM* MIEKE VON HOLM
Delicate, fragrant, dark pink flowers are held above upright foliage on slender stems.

***ONCOSTELE* CATATANTE ►**
Tall branching stems are smothered in small, long-lasting, terracotta blooms.

◄ *ONCOSTELE* MIDNIGHT MIRACLES 'MASSAI RED'
A more compact variety, with striking, upright sprays of star-like, deep burgundy flowers.

TOP FIVE
MULTI-PLANT DISPLAY IDEAS

Grouping together flowering orchids not only increases their visual impact, but also improves the growing conditions for the plants by creating a humid microclimate that they enjoy.

Aim for contrasts of colour and shape

1

STANDING PLANTS TOGETHER

Simply positioning orchids together creates a display with real impact, and helps to increase humidity in the surrounding air. Choose orchids that enjoy the same conditions, or combine them with other plants, such as ferns and bromeliads, for a tropical look.

Try moth orchids, see pp.114–117, *Dendrobium Polar Fire*, see pp.64–65, and warm-growing slipper orchids, see pp.108–111.

2

LARGE PLANTERS

Produce a spectacular centrepiece by placing several orchids in a large ornamental bowl, or planter, deep enough to house their pots. Finish with a decorative covering of moss. Remove the plants for watering, to avoid water accumulating in the base of the bowl.

Try moth orchids, see pp.114–117.

Group of the same orchid makes an impactful display

STANDS

Where space is limited, display stands with shelves or pot holders are a great way to show off your orchids. They can be positioned to provide plants with the right seasonal light levels and temperature, and prevent them being trapped behind curtains on cold nights.

Try oncidiums, see pp.98–101, or moth orchids, see pp.114–117.

Move plants around to best display those in flower

A glass terrarium allows close observation of miniatures

TERRARIUMS

A small, purpose-made terrarium, or even an old fish bowl or aquarium, makes the perfect warm, humid environment for miniature orchids. Position the orchids in their pots, or mounted on bark, and add attractive pieces of wood, stone, moss, and bark, together with small foliage plants, to create a naturalistic setting.

Try *Restrepia cuprea*, see pp.130–131, *Epidendrum porpax*, see p.79, and kite orchids, see pp.86–87.

GROWING CASES

Larger orchids look impressive growing in a glass case, which can vary in size and style to suit your space. Cases create a warm, humid microclimate, and this can be tailored to suit particular orchids, especially with climate controls to adjust the temperature, humidity, and light inside.

Try *Bulbophyllum lobbii*, see pp.44–45, *Vanda* Blue Magic, see pp.136–137, or *Zygopetalum* Artur Elle, see pp.140–141.

WARM-GROWING SLIPPER ORCHID

Paphiopedilum Maudiae

Exotic and extraordinary, this slipper-shaped flower stands above attractive patterned leaves, and is a great, easy-to-grow Paphiopedilum for beginners.

‖‖‖

VITAL STATISTICS

HOW IT GROWS As a sympodial terrestrial orchid, in damp soils and shady conditions.

ORIGIN Native to low altitude rainforests in Southeast Asia

ANATOMY Forms a cluster of connected leaf shoots, but no pseudobulbs. Flower stems grow up from the centre of the mottled leaves.

SIZE Flower stems reach 40cm (16in) tall, above low-growing leaves no more than 10cm (4in) high. Plants will spread to 20cm (8in) wide.

40cm (16in)

20cm (8in)

WATER

Water from the top of the pot and allow to drain well, do not stand in water. These orchids like to be damp most of the time, so check and water when the compost is starting to dry out. Mist the leaves regularly to create humidity.

POSITION

This orchid requires a warm room with a winter minimum of 18°C (64°F) and a shady spot in summer, to stop the mottled leaves burning, with a maximum of 25°C (77°F). Try a humid bathroom or kitchen where leaves can be misted regularly.

HELP TO FLOWER

Slipper orchids can be slow to re-flower, but this variety is more reliable. New flower stems come from the latest, matured rosette of leaves, so promoting strong new growth with correct feeding and watering should produce more flowers. Use a thin stake to help support the flower stem. When the flower drops, trim off the dead stem.

FEED

Use high-nitrogen fertilizer every 2–3 waterings while the new leaves are growing. Change to high-potash feed once the new leaves are maturing, to encourage the next flowering stem.

REPOT

Repot when the plant has increased in size to reach the edge of the pot. This is usually necessary every 2–3 years, or more often if it grows well. Wait until after flowering when the new leaf shoot starts to grow, and use medium bark chippings.

THE RELATIVES

THE RELATIVES

Warm-growing slipper orchids

The allure of these strange beauties, combined with their compact habit, and ease of cultivation, almost makes starting a collection irresistible. Where one flowers successfully, its relatives will too.

PAPHIOPEDILUM CALLOSUM ▶
A striking Southeast Asian species, with white-tipped purple and green flowers held above bold mottled leaves.

◀ **PAPHIOPEDILUM DELENATII**
A species from Vietnam, with rounded flowers up to 10cm (4in) across. Their shades of pastel pink are unusual among slipper orchids.

◄ PAPHIOPEDILUM PINOCCHIO
Compact and easy to care for, this variety blooms sequentially, with many blooms produced, one after another, from the same stem.

PAPHIOPEDILUM ►

SUKHAKULII
Native only to northern Thailand, this species readily produces dramaticially marked green and purple flowers.

◄ PAPHIOPEDILUM WARDII
This small, reliable species produces a 20cm (8in) tall flower stem from the centre of its mottled leaves, topped with a spectacularly patterned, green bloom.

COOL-GROWING SLIPPER ORCHID

Paphiopedilum insigne

Dramatic yellow-bronze flowers have long made this handsome species popular. Their rosettes of plain, pale-green leaves are typical of cool-growing slipper orchids.

VITAL STATISTICS

HOW IT GROWS This orchid has a sympodial habit and grows as a terrestrial, on damp, shady rainforest floors.

ORIGIN Native to high altitudes in Northern India.

ANATOMY Forms a cluster of connected leaf shoots, but no pseudobulbs. Tall flower stems emerge at the centre of the narrow leaves.

SIZE Leaves only reach 10cm (4in) high, but plants spread to 30cm (12in) wide. The stems, carrying a single flower, can grow up to 30cm (12in) tall.

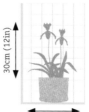

30cm (12in)

30cm (12in)

WATER

Water from the top of the pot and allow to drain well, but do not stand in water. These orchids like to be damp, so check the compost regularly and water when it is starting to dry out. Mist the leaves frequently to create humidity.

POSITION

Provide a cool room, such as a conservatory, with a minimum of 8°C (46°F) in winter. Find a shady spot in summer, to prevent direct light burning leaves, with temperatures no higher than 20°C (68°F); place outdoors if suitable.

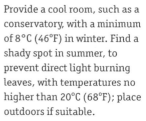

HELP TO FLOWER

Slipper orchids can be slow to re-flower, but this variety is more reliable than most. New single flowers come from the centre of the latest leaf rosettes, so promote strong growth with cool, humid conditions. When the flower drops, trim off the dead stem to the leaves. Use a thin stake to support the flower.

FEED

Use a high-nitrogen fertilizer every 2–3 waterings when the new leaves are growing. Use a high-potash fertilizer when the new set of leaves is maturing, to encourage the next flowering.

REPOT

Repot after flowering when the new leaf shoot starts to grow. This is usually necessary every 2–3 years, when the plant has grown to reach the edge of the pot, but sometimes more often if it is thriving. Use medium bark chippings.

THE RELATIVES

Other slipper orchids, with equally exotic flowers, also enjoy cool growing conditions.

PAPHIOPEDILUM LEEANUM
A hybrid with spectacular flowers, topped with a wide, sail-like white dorsal sepal with a characteristic central stripe.

PAPHIOPEDILUM VILLOSUM
Large, glossy, bronze flowers are held just above the plain green foliage.

MOTH ORCHID

Phalaenopsis Cool Breeze

This long-lasting, classic white moth orchid is easy to grow, will readily re-flower, and fits in with any décor. An essential part of any collection, it is a great beginner's orchid and an ideal gift.

ı ı

VITAL STATISTICS

HOW IT GROWS As a monopodial epiphyte, anchored to tree branches by strong aerial roots, with the leaves hanging down.

ORIGIN
Native to tropical Southeast Asia.

ANATOMY Fleshy leaves grow from a central crown. Thick roots grow inside and outside the pot. Flower stems emerge where leaves join the main stem.

SIZE Flower stems reach 50cm (20in) tall, while leaves in the basal rosette reach up to 20cm (8in) high, and spread to 40cm (16in) wide.

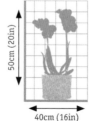

50cm (20in)

40cm (16in)

WATER

Water from the top of the pot and drain well. Do not stand in water. Water weekly in spring and summer, and every 2–3 weeks in autumn and winter, but check the pot is dry before watering. Mist aerial roots daily to increase humidity.

HELP TO FLOWER

Before the last of the main flush of flowers has dropped, trim the stem back above one of its pale nodes. Within 4–6 weeks, a side branch with new flower buds should grow from the node. Cut dead, brown stems back to the base. Move orchids that haven't flowered for over 6 months to a slightly cooler spot for a few weeks, and feed with a high-potash fertilizer. Stake stems to support the large flowers.

FEED

Use a high-nitrogen fertilizer every 2–3 waterings when the plant is just growing new leaves, or after repotting. Use a high-potash fertilizer when the leaves have grown, to encourage new flowers.

POSITION

This orchid requires a warm room with a minimum of 18°C (64°F) in winter, and a shady summer spot, with a maximum of 25°C (77°F). Any warm, light room would suit, where it can be admired.

REPOT

Repot when the pot is root-bound and if it is leaning over to one side. This is usually necessary every 2–3 years, and should be done after flowering. Use medium or coarse bark chippings. Lots of aerial roots indicate a happy plant, not necessarily that it needs repotting.

THE RELATIVES

Moth orchids

There are thousands of Phalaenopsis hybrids to choose from, in a glorious range of colours, patterns, and sizes. Along with some easily grown species, they all make ideal houseplants.

PHALAENOPSIS ATLANTIS ▶
These bright pink blooms last for several weeks and open in succession along stems about 50cm (20in) tall.

◀ PHALAENOPSIS CORNU-CERVI
A truly miniature moth orchid, with several small yellow and red patterned flowers, up to 5cm (2in) across, produced over many weeks.

◄ **PHALAENOPSIS EQUESTRIS**
This free-flowering, miniature
species bears delicate pink
blooms, up to 2.5cm (1in) wide,
on compact, branching stems.

PHALAENOPSIS HAPPY MINHO ▶
Unashamedly showy, with bold, pink
and white, candy-stripe flowers, this
hybrid creates a vibrant display.

◄ **PHALAENOPSIS LIMELIGHT**
The sunny yellow petals of this
popular hybrid make a striking
contrast with the magenta pink
lip at the centre of each flower.

SOUTH AMERICAN SLIPPER ORCHID

Phragmipedium besseae

Relatively newly discovered, this amazing species has incredibly bright orange-red flowers, with a slipper-shaped lip. It needs a warm, humid position to thrive.

VITAL STATISTICS

HOW IT GROWS As a sympodial terrestrial in damp shade, near streams and springs.

ORIGIN Found in Peru, Ecuador, and Colombia.

ANATOMY An orchid with a climbing habit, it has a long rhizome between the leaf shoots, but no pseudobulbs.

SIZE Elegant leaves reach 20cm (8in) in height, and plants spread to 30cm (12in) wide. Flowers are borne on stems up to 50cm (20in) tall.

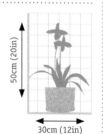

50cm (20in)

30cm (12in)

WATER
They like to be damp most of the time, so check weekly and water when the pot is starting to dry out. Mist leaves regularly to create humidity. Water from the top of the pot and allow to drain well. Do not stand in water.

POSITION
Give this orchid space in a warm room with a minimum of 18°C (54°F) in winter, and a shaded spot in summer with a maximum of 25°C (86°F). A humid bathroom or kitchen window, where the leaves can be misted regularly, can be ideal.

HELP TO FLOWER

Warmth, humidity, and the correct feeding will all promote strong new growth. These new rosettes of leaves will send up flower stems, which produce several blooms in succession. Trim spent flower stems back to the leaves. Staking will help to support the thin flower stems.

FEED

Use a high-nitrogen fertilizer at every other watering when the new leaves are growing. Switch to a high-potash fertilizer when the new leaves are maturing to promote flowering.

REPOT

Repot when the plant has reached the edge of the pot. This is usually every 2–3 years, or more often if it grows well. Repot after flowering, as the new leaf shoot emerges. Use rockwool potting medium.

THE RELATIVES

Phragmipedium species all like to be kept warm and damp, as they are naturally found by streams in tropical rainforests.

PHRAGMIPEDIUM SEDENII
This reliable old hybrid's white rounded flowers and softly blushed-pink slipper make it an attractive orchid to collect.

▼ **PHRAGMIPEDIUM GRANDE**
This impressive hybrid has large green flowers with incredibly long, pendent petals. Can reach 70cm (28in) high when in flower.

PLEIONE FORMOSANA

This small orchid is really easy to grow, which makes it ideal for beginners and children. It couldn't be simpler: if the plant has leaves it needs water and if it doesn't, keep dry.

VITAL STATISTICS

HOW IT GROWS As a terrestrial orchid, with a sympodial habit. It is found in damp soil, in shady woodland.

ORIGIN Native to the mountains of China and Taiwan.

ANATOMY Produces rounded, deciduous pseudobulbs, which die as the new one matures. Flower stems emerge from new shoots.

SIZE Flowers that reach 10cm (4in) high nestle among leaves that are 15cm (6in) tall. These small orchids spread about 10cm (4in) wide.

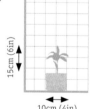

15cm (6in)

10cm (4in)

WATER

When the new shoots grow in spring, begin watering weekly and continue through summer to swell the new pseudobulbs. Mist leaves daily during summer. Once its leaves have dropped, this species needs a dry winter rest, so do not water in winter.

POSITION

Place outdoors in a shady spot during spring and summer; direct sun might burn the leaves, but they will drop in autumn. Before frosts arrive, move indoors into a very cool, bright room at 5–15°C (41–59°F) for the winter rest.

HELP TO FLOWER

A cold, dry winter rest encourages the next season's flowering. Blooms grow from the centre of the new leaf shoots in late winter and spring. When each flower has faded, trim its stem back just above the leaf.

FEED

Add a high-nitrogen fertilizer every 2–3 waterings in spring and summer to boost new growth. A high-potash fertilizer in late summer and autumn will promote flowering. No feeding is needed in winter.

REPOT

Annual repotting can be done in early spring as the new shoots start to grow. Remove old compost and older, dead pseudobulbs, and repot with a mix of fine bark, perlite, and houseplant compost, or a similar mix that will keep the roots moist all summer.

"Once its leaves have dropped, this species needs a dry winter rest, so don't water in winter."

THE RELATIVES

THE RELATIVES

Pleione

The many attractive Pleione hybrids available provide a wide variety of flower colours, but are all compact and deciduous, and require the same simple care to thrive.

PLEIONE BULBOCODIOIDES ▶
Native to China, Nepal, and Taiwan, this species' pink flowers have white-frilled lips, and are borne on upright stems.

**◀ PLEIONE FORMOSANA
VAR. ALBA**
This is the elegant, pure white, albino form of the popular pink species. There is just a touch of yellow in the flower's throat.

◀ PLEIONE PITON
Upright stems support large
flowers, in a soft shade of
lavender, with bold purple
patterning on their lip.

PLEIONE PLEIONOIDES ▶
This species has a distinctive,
broad, rich-pink lip. The petals
and sepals are narrower and
vary from lilac to dark pink.

◀ PLEIONE SHANTUNG
While many pleiones are shades
of pink and purple, this renowned
variety is an unusual hue of pale
lemon yellow.

TOP FIVE

HANGING DISPLAY IDEAS

When other surfaces are full, find more space for orchids by suspending them from the wall or ceiling, where they will enjoy the extra light and air movement as they would in the rainforest.

1

HANGING POTS

With the addition of secure plastic, metal, or rope pot hangers, any potted orchid will look fabulous hung from a hook or bracket. Most orchids will flourish provided the container has plenty of drainage holes, but it particularly suits those with pendent flower stems.

Try a rag orchid, see pp.54–57; chain orchid, see pp.72–73; or *Cymbidium* Sarah Jean 'Ice Cascade', see p.61.

Many containers can be converted to hanging pots

As the orchid grows its roots will begin to poke through

2

KOKEDAMA

This quirky Japanese method of growing plants involves wrapping the roots up into a ball with sphagnum moss. This is then finished with a decorative layer of moss, and secured and suspended with fishing line or jute string. Water by submerging the ball briefly when it has dried out.

Try with a moth orchid, see pp.114–117.

3

HANGING BASKETS

Orchids are often grown in slatted wooden baskets, but any basket with lots of holes or an open structure can be used. Hanging baskets particularly suit larger specimens that enjoy good drainage, and those that produce flower stems from underneath the plant.

Try an upside-down orchid, see pp.132–133; pineapple orchid, see pp.68–69; or *Dracula bella*, see pp.76–77.

The unusual flowers of Dracula bella hang down from the base

4

GROWING WITH BARE ROOTS

The aerial root systems of epiphytic orchids flourish without a pot, and make a dramatic feature when the plant is suspended from a high hook by a wire or string hanger. Attach the hanger to the base of the plant, where there is often a small plastic basket, and mist the roots daily.

Try *Vanda* Blue Magic, see pp.136–137.

Convert an old shutter into a display board

5

VERTICAL DISPLAYS

Make imaginative use of walls, shelving, or shutters to generate new display spaces. Hang mounted or potted plants from hooks or brackets, as well as placing them on shelves, to create a spectacular, ever-changing theatre of plants in flower.

Try with a corsage orchid, see pp.48–51; rag orchid, see pp.54–57; or *Zygopetalum* Artur Elle, see pp.140–141.

A mass of aerial roots makes a bold visual statement

PLEUROTHALLIS RESTREPIOIDES

This fascinating free-flowering species holds its many attractive red and white patterned flowers, on elegant, arching stems. It will flower reliably if kept cool and moist throughout summer.

VITAL STATISTICS

HOW IT GROWS As a sympodial epiphyte, on the branches of trees, at high altitude.

ORIGIN Found in cloud forests from Colombia to Peru.

ANATOMY Thick, rounded leaves grow from spindly stems. Flower stems and keikis arise at the joint between leaf and stem.

SIZE The rounded leaves can reach 25cm (10in) long, and will spread into a clump 20cm (8in) wide. Arching flower stems are 30cm (12in) tall.

30cm (12in)

20cm (8in)

WATER

Water from above, and do not stand the pot in water. Grow in sphagnum moss, as this reatins moisture around the roots. Check the pot weekly and water when drying out. Mist the leaves regularly to create humidity.

POSITION

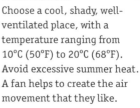

Choose a cool, shady, well-ventilated place, with a temperature ranging from 10°C (50°F) to 20°C (68°F). Avoid excessive summer heat. A fan helps to create the air movement that they like.

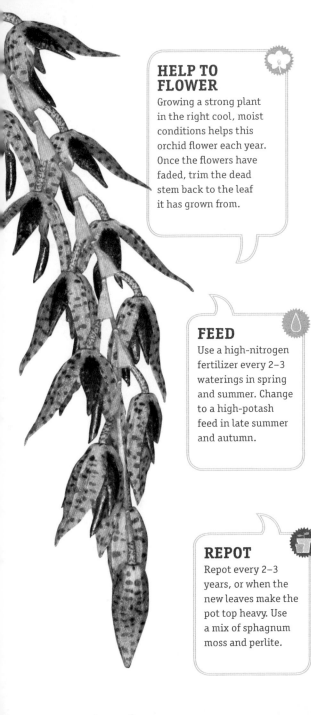

HELP TO FLOWER

Growing a strong plant in the right cool, moist conditions helps this orchid flower each year. Once the flowers have faded, trim the dead stem back to the leaf it has grown from.

FEED

Use a high-nitrogen fertilizer every 2–3 waterings in spring and summer. Change to a high-potash feed in late summer and autumn.

REPOT

Repot every 2–3 years, or when the new leaves make the pot top heavy. Use a mix of sphagnum moss and perlite.

THE RELATIVES

Similar cool, humid conditions also suit these striking *Pleurothallis* species, which will often thrive in a terrarium.

PLEUROTHALLIS TRUNCATA
Each spray of tiny bright orange, ball-shaped flowers is perfectly displayed laid on top of a leaf.

PLEUROTHALLIS PALLIOLATA
This strange single flower sits on the heart-shaped leaf, and has been likened to an open-mouthed baby bird.

OCTOPUS ORCHID

Prosthechea cochleata

The cute blooms on this national flower of Belize look just like a little octopus, but it is also known as the "cockleshell orchid" due to the shell-shaped lip at the top of the flower. It's an easy beginner's orchid.

VITAL STATISTICS

HOW IT GROWS This orchid has a sympodial habit. It grows as an epiphyte on tree branches, with aerial roots to anchor it.

ORIGIN From Central America and northern South America.

ANATOMY Produces oval pseudobulbs, with a pair of broad, dark-green leaves at each tip. The flower stem emerges from between the leaves.

SIZE Flower stems reach 40cm (16in) high, with leaves up to 30cm (12in) tall. Plants spread to 20cm (8in) wide.

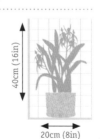

40cm (16in)

20cm (8in)

WATER

Water from the top of the pot and allow the plant to drain well so that it does not stand in water. In spring and summer water weekly, and every 2–3 weeks in autumn and winter, but always check that the pot is dry first. Mist the leaves daily to increase humidity.

POSITION

Place in a cool room with a minimum of 10°C (50°F) in winter, and a maximum of 20°C (68°F) in summer, when it will also need shade. Try a humid bathroom or kitchen, where leaves can be misted regularly.

HELP TO FLOWER

Providing cooler winter conditions, and the correct feeding and watering to form a strong new pseudobulb will encourage re-flowering each year on the matured bulb. When the flowers are over, trim off the dead stems.

FEED

Use a high-nitrogen fertilizer every 2–3 waterings while the new pseudobulbs and leaves are forming. Use a high-potash feed to fatten-up the pseudobulb and promote flowering.

REPOT

Repot when the pseudobulbs reach the edge of the pot. This is usually needed every 2–3 years. Wait until after flowering, when the new leaf shoot starts to emerge. Use medium or coarse bark chippings.

THE RELATIVES

These other *Prosthechea* species are also easy to grow and free-flowering, so make excellent beginner's orchids.

PROSTHECHEA RADIATA
A robust plant with heads of long-lasting, highly fragrant, ice-green flowers in the summer.

PROSTHECHEA GARCIANA
A compact species with pairs of back-to-back speckled pink flowers, which are also highly fragrant.

RESTREPIA CUPREA

A true miniature orchid, this species has amazing tiny, boat-shaped flowers in an almost metallic shade of copper. Its diminutive size makes it ideal to grow in a terrarium as part of a miniature orchid garden.

VITAL STATISTICS

HOW IT GROWS As an epiphyte with a spreading sympodial habit, clinging to small branches in cloud forests.

ORIGIN Native to the mountains of Colombia.

ANATOMY Forms a clump of spindly stems with small, thick leaves. Where leaves join stems, flowers arise, and keikis can grow too.

SIZE Leaves only reach 10cm (4in) tall on these small plants, with the flowers held at a similar height. Plants will spread to 10cm (4in) in time.

10cm (4in)

10cm (4in)

WATER

These orchids grow best in sphagnum moss, which helps the roots stay constantly moist. Check weekly and water when drying out. Water from above, and never stand in water. Mist leaves regularly to create humidity.

POSITION

Choose a cool, shady, well-ventilated place, with a temperature range of 10–20°C (50–68°F). Ensure that they stay cool in summer. Create the air movement that they like with a fan.

HELP TO FLOWER

The flowering season is variable, and strong specimens grown in cool, shady, moist conditions should re-flower easily through the year. After flowers have faded, trim the dead stem back to where it joins the leaf.

FEED

Use a high-nitrogen feed every 2–3 waterings in spring and summer, then a high-potash feed in late summer and autumn.

THE RELATIVES

All compact and great value, *Restrepia* species thrive on a cool windowsill and are free-flowering throughout the year.

RESTREPIA GUTULLATA
Use a magnifying glass to really appreciate the deep-red spots and stripes on this incredible little flower.

RESTREPIA BRACHYPUS
The small, yellow flowers of this South American species are dramatically striped with dark red.

REPOT

Repot every 2–3 years or when the new leaves are making the small pot top heavy. Use a mix of sphagnum moss and perlite.

1

ORCHID

eff132

Orchid profiles

UPSIDE-DOWN ORCHID

Stanhopea tigrina

Best grown in a hanging basket, this orchid earns its "upside-down" reputation with downward-growing stems of fragrant, short-lived blooms.

VITAL STATISTICS

HOW IT GROWS As a sympodial epiphyte on the branches of trees, with aerial roots to anchor it.

ORIGIN Native to Mexico.

ANATOMY Each round pseudobulb produces a single leaf at its tip. The long flower stems grow downwards.

SIZE The upright leaves reach 40cm (16in) tall and plants can spread to 30cm (12in) wide. Long flower stems hang down 20cm (8in) below the plant.

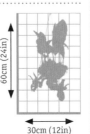

60cm (24in)

30cm (12in)

WATER

Water from the top of the basket and drain well, never leaving it standing in water. Always check the compost is dry before watering. Water once or twice a week in spring and summer, and every 1–2 weeks in autumn and winter. Mist the leaves daily to increase humidity levels around the plant.

POSITION

Place in good light, in a room with a cool temperature ranging from a minimum of 10°C (50°F) in winter, to a summer maximum of 20°C (68°F). Shade leaves from direct summer sun. Try a humid bathroom or kitchen, where leaves can be misted daily.

HELP TO FLOWER

A cooler winter, and correct feeding and watering, will form a new pseudobulb that is ready to flower. Ensure flower stems can grow down without catching on roots or the basket slats.

FEED

Use a high-nitrogen fertilizer every 2–3 waterings during the growing season, as new leaves and bulbs are being formed. Swap to a high-potash fertilizer when the pseudobulb is fattening up, to encourage flowering.

REPOT

Every 2–3 years, when the new pseudobulbs reach the edge of the basket, it is time to repot. Wait until after flowering, when new leaf growth begins. Add sphagnum moss to medium bark chippings to help retain moisture.

THE RELATIVES

These spectacular species also produce many exotic flowers hanging beneath the plant on long stems.

STANHOPEA OCULATA
Pendent stems bear large, yellow, speckled flowers, with a black eye at their centre and a heavy scent.

STANHOPEA GRAVEOLENS
This Central American species produces several waxy, bold yellow and orange, fragrant flowers on each large stem.

THUNIA GATTONENSIS

These deciduous orchids rest during winter and grow rapidly in summer, producing attractive soft leaves along tall stems. These culminate in a cluster of delicate, white, tissue-like flowers.

VITAL STATISTICS

HOW IT GROWS This is a sympodial orchid, which grows as a terrestrial in damp soil, in shady woodland.

ORIGIN Native to Southeast Asia.

ANATOMY Forms deciduous, cane-like pseudobulbs. Flower stems grow from the top of new canes, and any older pseudobulbs die.

SIZE Slim canes reach 80cm (32in) high when flowering, with numerous pointed leaves along their length. Clumps spread to 30cm (12in) wide.

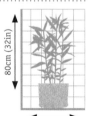

80cm (32in)

30cm (12in)

WATER

This species needs a dry winter rest, so do not water once the leaves have dropped. When the new shoots begin to grow in spring, start watering weekly, and continue through summer, as the new cane-like pseudobulbs grow. Mist leaves daily in summer.

POSITION

Keep in a cool room in spring and summer, with a maximum of 15°C (59°F), shaded from the heat of direct sunlight. Choose a cool, light room in winter (minimum 8°C/46°F).

HELP TO FLOWER

A cold, dry winter rest encourages these orchids to produce flowers the following season. The flowers are short-lived, only blooming for about a week. When the flowers at the top of the cane have faded, trim their dead stems back to the leaves.

FEED

Apply a high-nitrogen fertilizer with every 2–3 waterings in spring and summer. Swap to a high-potash fertilizer in late summer. Do not feed during winter.

REPOT

Repot annually in early spring, as new shoots emerge. Remove dead pseudobulbs, and repot with a moisture retentive mix of fine bark, perlite, and houseplant compost.

THE RELATIVES

These *Thunia* species also thrive in cool conditions. Their graceful blooms are short-lived, but always a delight.

THUNIA MARSHALLIANA
A showy species from Myanmar, Thailand, and southern China, with a bright orange lip, which contrasts with the pure white petals and sepals.

THUNIA ALBA
Almost pure white, the blooms of this Southeast Asian species have just a touch of yellow at their centre.

VANDA

Vanda Blue Magic

Stunning violet-blue flowers make this large hybrid incredibly popular. It thrives given warmth and high humidity, and in ideal conditions will grow with its aerial roots loose or displayed in a vase.

VITAL STATISTICS

HOW IT GROWS This monopodial orchid grows at high altitude, as an epiphyte on the branches of forest trees.

ORIGIN Native to cloud forests from Colombia to Peru.

ANATOMY Thick leaves fan out from spindly stems. Flower stems arise where stems and leaves join, and keikis can grow from there too.

SIZE Plants in flower can reach 60cm (24in) tall, and even 100cm (40in) including the long aerial roots. Foliage can spread to 40cm (16in) wide.

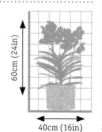

60cm (24in)

40cm (16in)

FEED

When the plant is just growing new leaves, or after repotting, use a high-nitrogen fertilizer every 2–3 waterings. Use a high-potash fertilizer to encourage flowering once the leaf growth has finished. Add feed to spray water and apply when misting the roots.

POSITION

Place in a warm room with a minimum of 18°C (64°F) in winter and a maximum of 30°C (86°F) in summer, when it needs plenty of light. Find a warm, light room where regular spraying can create extra humidity.

HELP TO FLOWER

Good light and feeding with a high-potash fertilizer will encourage new flowers, in any season. Staking may be needed if growing in a pot. When the flowers have finished, trim the stem back to the leaves.

WATER

However you choose to grow your *Vanda*, always mist its aerial roots daily.
In a pot: Water from the top and drain well. When the pot is dry, water weekly in spring and summer, and every 2–3 weeks in autumn and winter.
Growing with loose aerial roots: Spray the aerial roots well every 1–2 days, so they turn from grey to green.
In a vase: Create humidity by tucking the roots into a glass vase. Pour water over them twice a week, leave for 10 minutes, then tip it out.

REPOT

If growing in a pot, repot after flowering, using coarse bark chippings, when the pot is root-bound and the plant is becoming top heavy. This is usually necessary every 2–3 years. Lots of aerial roots is a sign of a happy plant and may not mean it needs repotting.

THE RELATIVES

Vanda

Vibrant and exotic, the speckled flowers of the Vanda family come in a spectacular range of colours. Just be sure to provide a warm, humid environment, and they will thrive.

VANDA EXOTIC PURPLE ▶
Dazzling flowers, their wide petals boldly patterned in purple and white, make this an extremely popular Vanda hybrid.

◀ VANDA ROTHSCHILDIANA
The large, pale violet-blue flowers of this tall hybrid reach 10cm (4in) across, and have an attractive dark purple lip.

◄ *VANDA* PINK MAGIC
*This striking hybrid boasts large,
long-lasting flowers, in an
arresting shade of vibrant pink,
with a pale mottled pattern.*

**_VANDA_ PRINCESS ►
MIKASA BLUE**
*A hybrid with smaller, deep
lavender-blue flowers, each
about 6cm (2.5in) across.*

◄ *VANDA* YELLOW MAGIC
*An unusual yellow variety, with
dark red spots peppering its large
blooms. Warm, humid conditions
are essential for it to flourish.*

ZYGOPETALUM ARTUR ELLE

An unusual combination of purple and green creates striking blooms with the added bonus of sweet fragrance, making this easy orchid a must for any collector.

VITAL STATISTICS

HOW IT GROWS As a sympodial epiphyte on tree branches, with strong aerial roots to anchor it.

ORIGIN From the rainforests of South America.

ANATOMY Forms large, rounded pseudobulbs, with leaves produced at their tips. The flower stem grows within the new leaf shoot.

SIZE Leaves growing at the tips of pseudobulbs reach 30cm (12in) tall, and plants spread to 20cm (8in) wide. Flower stems can be 40cm (16in) high.

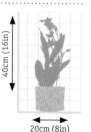

40cm (16in)

20cm (8in)

WATER

Water from the top of the pot and allow to drain well, never leaving the pot standing in water. Allow the pot to dry out in between waterings. Water weekly in spring and summer, and every 2–3 weeks in autumn and winter.

POSITION

Place in good, indirect light, in a room with an intermediate temperature range: a winter minimum of 12°C (54°F) to a summer maximum of 20°C (68°F). Try a humid bathroom or kitchen, where it's easy to keep leaves misted regularly.

HELP TO FLOWER

Given the correct levels of light and humidity, this orchid should flower happily each year. The flowering season is naturally variable, depending on when the plant starts into growth. When the flowers are spent, trim the dead stems off.

FEED

Use a high-nitrogen feed every 2–3 waterings when new leaves are growing. As the new pseudobulb matures, swap to a high-potash feed to promote blooms.

REPOT

It is time to repot when new pseudobulbs reach the edge of the pot. This is usually every 2–3 years. Repot after flowering, when the new leaf shoot starts to grow. Use coarse or medium bark chippings.

THE RELATIVES

Although *Zygopetalum* hybrids are more commonly cultivated, these interesting species are just as easy to grow.

ZYGOPETALUM CRINITUM

This Brazilian species is compact and easy to grow. Its highly fragrant flowers have dramatic purple markings.

ZYGOPETALUM MACKAYI

A spectacular species, with tall stems of large, heavily scented flowers, in contrasting shades of purple, white, and green.

INDEX

ABOUT THE AUTHOR

Sara Rittershausen runs the top orchid nursery in the UK, Burnham Nurseries in Devon, which was started by her grandfather and continued by his daughter Wilma and son Brian (Sara's dad). Sara has played a role in several orchid books, is an RHS Orchid Judge on the Orchid Committee, President of the Devon Orchid Society, and has been involved in many of Burnham Nurseries' Gold Medal-winning exhibits, including at the Chelsea Flower Show and other RHS shows through the years. At the London Orchid Show 2018, Burnham Nurseries won a gold medal for its display, the seventh year in a row.

ACKNOWLEDGEMENTS

DK would like to thank Marie Lorimer for indexing, Jane Simmonds for proofreading, and the following DTP Designers at DK Delhi for creating the image cut-outs: Satish Chandra Gaur, Rajdeep Singh, Anurag Trivedi.

Picture credits

The publisher would like to thank the following for their kind permission to reproduce their photographs:

(Key: a-above; b-below/bottom; c-centre; f-far; l-left; r-right; t-top)

123RF.com: Ariadna126 8cb, 78bc, 79l; Whiskybottle 6çb (Red-Spotted Lip Cymbidium Orchid), 7tr, 60cr, 68bc, 69tl. **Alamy Stock Photo**: AfriPics.com 7br, 20clb, 75l; Avalon / Photoshot License 4cra, 37l, 70cb; Zena Elea 5clb, 41cra; Gabbro 13bc, 139cr; Garden World Images Ltd 5bl, 13clb, 41crb, 135cra; John Glover 6ca, 58bc, 59l; Alan Gregg 9tc, 13cla, 92cr, 134bc, 134-135; Glenn Harper 13br, 141crb; Rex May 47cra; RM Floral 13bl, 135crb; Scenics & Science 8tl, 75cra; Vario images GmbH & Co.KG 8tr, 83; Xinhua 8bl, 77cra. **Dorling Kindersley**: Brian North / RHS Chelsea Flower 5cb, 43crb; RHS Malvern Flower Show 2014 12bl, 123clb; RHS Wisley 6cb, 12clb, 57cla, 123cr. **Dreamstime.com**: Surachet Khamsuk 18bl, 34bc, 36bc, 38bc, 40bc, 42bc, 44bc, 46bc, 48bc, 54bc, 58bc, 62bc, 64bc, 66bc, 68bc, 70cr, 72bc, 74bc, 76bc, 78bc, 80bc, 82bc, 84bc, 86bc, 90bc, 94bc, 96bc, 98bc, 102bc, 108bc, 112bc, 114bc, 118bc, 120bc, 126bc, 128bc, 130bc, 134bc, 136bc, 140bc; Whiskybottle 8cra, 84bc, 85l. **Getty Images**: Wagner Campelo 10clb, 101cla; I love Photo and Apple 5cb (Calanthe), 46bc, 47l; Jouan / Rius / Gamma-Rapho 4ca, 35l; Kevin Schafer 8bc, 81crb. **naturepl.com**: Chris Mattison 5bc, 44bc, 45l, 71cr. **Henry Oakeley**: 4cb, 4bc, 4br, 6tr, 6cra, 6clb, 7crb, 7bc, 8cla, 8cb (*Laelia gouldiana*), 8bc (*Epidendrum porpax*), 9tc (*Maxillaria variabilis*), 9cla, 9ca, 9cb, 9bl, 11bc, 12tc, 12ca, 12br, 13tl, 35cra, 35crb, 37crb, 61cla, 61cr, 67crb, 73crb, 75crb, 79cra, 81cra, 87cra, 91l, 92bl, 93cla, 93bl, 127l, 133cra, 133crb. **Rex by Shutterstock**: Amy Sancetta / AP 5ca, 43cra; Paul Brown 5tl, 38bc, 39l. **Sara Rittershausen**: 4crb, 5tc, 5ca (*Bulbophyllum ambrosia*), 6tc, 6ca (*Coelogyne massangeana*), 6crb, 6bc, 7cra, 8ca, 9cb (*Miltonia spectabilis*), 9bc, 9bc (*Miltonia flavescens*), 10tl, 10cra, 11tl, 11tc, 11cla, 11cra, 12tr, 12ca (*Prosthechea radiata*), 12cb, 12cb (*Prosthechea garciana*), 12bc, 37cra, 45cra, 45crb, 57bc, 60bl, 61bl, 73cra, 77crb, 93cr, 95cra, 95crb, 110bl, 111bl, 113l, 117cla, 119br, 127cra, 127crb, 129cra, 129crb, 131cra. **Science Photo Library**: Paul Harcourt Davies 9clb, 87crb; Sam K Tran 5tr, 47crb.

Cover images: *Front*: **Getty Images**: FrankvandenBergh b; *Back*: **Dreamstime.com**: Fwstupidio cr; *Spine*: **Getty Images**: FrankvandenBergh t.

Endpaper images: *Front*: **Dreamstime.com**: Surachet Khamsuk cla, clb, c, bc, cra, crb.

All other images © Dorling Kindersley
For further information see: www.dkimages.com